AN ILLUSTRATED SOURCEBOOK ON THE HOLOCAUST

VOLUME 1

AN ILLUSTRATED SOURCEBOOK ON THE HOLOCAUST

VOLUME 1

By Zosa Szajkowski

KTAV PUBLISHING HOUSE, INC.
NEW YORK
1977

Library of Congress Cataloging in Publication Data

Szajkowski, Zosa, 1911-
 An illustrated sourcebook on the Holocaust.

 Bibliography: v. 1, p.
 Includes index.
1. Holocaust, Jewish (1939-1945)—Pictorial works. 2.
Antisemitism—Germany—Pictorial works. 3. Germany—
Politics and government—1933-1945— Pictorial works.
I. Title.
D810.J4S933   940.53′1503′924   77-5350
ISBN 0-87068-294-6 (v. 1)

MANUFACTURED IN THE UNITED STATES OF AMERICA

CONTENTS

INTRODUCTION

This book, the first of three volumes, is not an illustrated history of the Holocaust. Rather, it is a collection of illustrations of certain aspects of such a history.

The materials reproduced in the pages that follow were not secret or confidential. They were easily available to the public in Germany as well as in the occupied territories and neutral countries during World War II. The volume is, then, a collection of visual materials on events that were familiar to every man, woman, and child, of every social group.

Let us imagine, for the sake of speculative argument, that the Germans and other peoples during World War II knew nothing about the horrors taking place in the concentration camps, and about the Nazi final solution to the Jewish problem. Even if this had been so, it would have been impossible for them not to see or hear the daily anti-Jewish propaganda, and to witness at least some of the practical steps that led to the killing of six million Jews.

As the illustrations in this volume demonstrate, the populace of Germany and German occupied countries learned about these matters in the streets, cafes, restaurants, and shops; at exhibitions, theatres, movies, and sporting events; through speeches on the radio and at meetings; through newspapers, magazines, and books. It was well-nigh impossible to take a step without coming across notices that trains, stores, restaurants, parks, baths, and other public facilities were reserved for Aryans only. The people of Germany must have seen the destroyed synagogues, the yellow badges worn by the Jews, the deportations of the Jews, the many small and large camps located near their towns and cities. How could they have failed to ask themselves what had happened to their deported Jewish neighbors, or to what end the anti-Jewish propaganda and other measures were leading?

The materials in this collection also illustrate the complicity of antisemites outside Germany before and during World War II. Surely much of the propaganda material in the occupied and neutral countries was instigated by the German propaganda machinery, but a part of it was of purely local origin. With the arrival of the German armies, antisemites in France, Lithuania, Poland, Rumania, and other countries progressed from their relatively mild anti-Jewish propaganda and small-scale pogroms to active participation in the German final solution of the Jewish problem, often without having a clear-cut idea of the steps in this solution.

The collaboration of non-Germans in the persecution of the Jews, and their active involvement in the anti-Jewish propaganda, in the economic ruination of the Jews, the take-overs of Jewish properties, and the internment and deportation of Jews, were all a result of the prewar antisemitism. This collaboration by non-Germans made Hitler's task easier, both in the general conduct of the war and in the final solution of the Jewish problem. This collaboration by non-Germans—not merely individuals, but large masses of the populace—should become an integral part of the historiography of the Holocaust, though without minimizing the German initiative and leading role in the massacre of six million Jews.

Critics may put forward the argument that it is unwise to publish this collection, because the anti-Jewish materials it contains will be utilized by neo-Nazis in Germany and antisemites in other countries. In response to this I should like to relate a personal experience.

In 1945 I was serving with the 82nd Airborne Division of the U.S. Army in Berlin. One Sunday afternoon I was walking with another soldier along the Unter den Linden. We noticed two beautiful girls; one had a concentration-camp number tattooed on her arm, the other was wearing a long-sleeved blouse. We started a conversation and learned that they were both German Jewesses. I asked the girl with the long-sleeved blouse: "Why are you hiding your lovely arms?" She began to cry. The other girl told us about her many discussions with her friend on this very subject. "She is ashamed and afraid because of the tattoo, as if she were not the victim but the criminal." They must have continued the discussion after we left them, because the next time we met, they were wearing kerchiefs made of yellow material marked with the Jewish badge and the arms of both were sleeveless. They removed their kerchiefs and waved them at us as if they were flags. Both girls were completely liberated from fear and feelings of shame. The tattooed numbers had become a symbol of pride. We embraced and laughed, while the Germans around us looked on, ashamed and respectful.

Zosa Szajkowski

New York City
Summer 1976

I. **PRELUDE**

(1) "The National Socialists and National Germans against each other—and against the Jews," montage of electoral posters and cartoons in the *Central Verein-Zeitung*, November 11, 1932.

2

Die Generalpumpe Europas, Familie Rothschild, hatte auch in Oesterreich eine Filiale. Der Wiener Vertreter dieser sauberen Gemeinschaft sitzt nun allerdings in Dachau. Es ist dafür Sorge getragen, daß ihn die Mitgefangenen nicht um hochverzinsliche Darlehen anpumpen können. Zeitgenössische Karikatur um 1800.

2

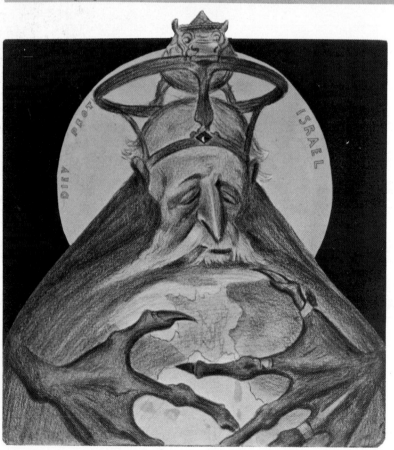

3

(2) A cartoon of ca. 1800 against the Rothschilds, reproduced in *Flammenzeichen* (Stuttgart), May 1938. (3) An 1898 French cartoon by C. Léandre at the time of the Dreyfus Affair; reproduced by Dr. R. W. Stock in a book published by the *Stürmer* in 1939.

GUESTS AT THE ABBEY

It wasn't such a long business as this, Finkelstein, liquidating the Czar.

6

We don't let our DOGS do that.

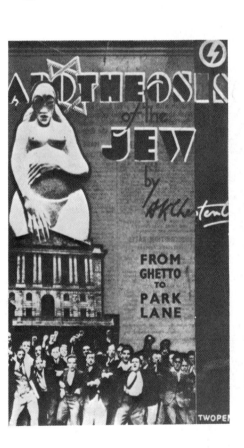

5

4

(4) Cover of A. K. Chesterton's antisemitic pamphlet, London. (5) Antisemitic pamphlet published by the Imperial Fascist League of England, April 1936. (6) Antisemitic cartoon in the *Free Press* of London, May–June 1937; used by the *Stürmer*.

Siegfried-Line-Song.

Here is the right version of the Siegfried-Line-Song,
by permission of Kennedy & Carr, Moody & Sankey.

We'd like to get our jobs back on the home-front line,
Can you live upon your pension, Mother dear?
We'd like to get our jobs back on the home-front line,
From Jew-boys in the rear!
Whether our children eat or starve,
Jews just rub along without a care.
We'd like to get our jobs back on the home-front line,
For we think we've done our share.

It's all right hanging washing on the Siegfried Line,
If you've got a change of clothing you-can spare,
It's all right hanging washing on the Siegfried Line,
If Yiddish clothes would wear.
Whether the weather's wet or fine,
They just seem like shoddy Jewish wear,
We'll try to hang the washing on the Siegfried Line,
If our clothes last out till there.

We're not so sure that laundering is our proper job,
If it is, we'd like to wash our things at home,
We're not so sure that laundering is our proper job,
So far away from home.
Whether Belisha pays his bob, or not
Or just lets us pay the lion's share,
We're not so sure that laundering is our proper job,
'Cos the wages aren't quite fair!

8

7

BOLSHEVIK

TURN ME OVER

10

What did Britain get out of the last War?
Nothing.   (over a million dead etc)
What did Germany get out of the last war?
Nothing.   (over 2 million dead etc)
Then who did gain out of the last War?
          THE JEWS!
Money, Business and our Heritage.
Refuse to fight again for Jew interests
          PERISH JUDAH!

9

(7) A woman selling an antisemitic magazine in the streets of London in 1937; published in the *Völkischer Beobachter* of November 24, 1938. **(8)** Antisemitic song sang at a London meeting of Oswald Mosley on August 30, 1939; used by the German propaganda in 1941. **(9–10)** Two antisemitic stickers distributed in London before the outbreak of World War II.

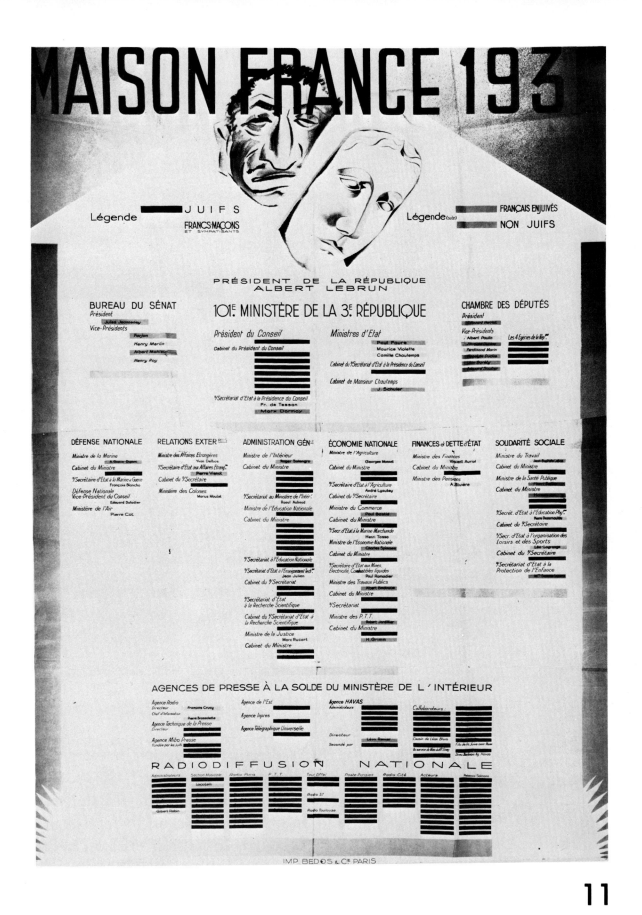

(11) A French poster showing that most ministries, the press, and the radio were presumably controlled by Jews, Freemasons, and their sympathizers, 1936.

18

Les juifs à bas
Le Coq vivra!
___
De joden uit de baan
Welvaart in den haan

De Joden zijn ons ongeluk

Koopt NIET
bij Joden
Koopt bij
Volksgenooten

Lees VOLKSVERWERING

17

13

14

L'adoration du veau d'or selon le rite judéo-socialiste
REGARDEZ A LA LOUPE, VICTIMES DES POLITICO FINANCIERS
IDENTIFIEZ CES POLITICIENS ET VOUS DÉCOUVREZ LA
BANDE DE CARTOUCHE NI LES ASSOCIÉS SE
COUVRENT DE TOUTES LES COULEURS POLITIQUES

15

12

Les Juifs
à la porte
Travail aux Belges

16

(12) "Jews out," a sticker on the synagogue of Turkish Jews in Antwerp, 1938. (13–14) Anti-Jewish propaganda in Belgium in the form of one-way tickets to Jerusalem, "3rd class convoy of cattle," 1938. (15) Pre-war poster against Jews and Socialists in Belgium. (16–19) Pre-war anti-Jewish stickers, Belgium.

La confiscation de tous les biens que les Juifs ont volés aux Belges comblerait nos déficits budgétaires.

19

24

21

22

20

23

(20) A pre-war Belgian edition of the *Protocols of the Elders of Zion*. **(21)** Belgian antisemitic cartoon against the French Front Populaire, *Pays Réel*, April 6, 1938. **(22)** Pre-war antisemitic poster of the Norwegian Najonal Samling movement. **(23)** Cartoon against Jews and Freemasons in the *Nation-en*, Stockholm. **(24)** Cartoon in *Front National* of Switzerland against stores owned by Jews, June 13, 1936.

8

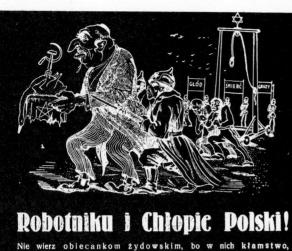

Robotniku i Chłopie Polski!

Nie wierz obiecankom żydowskim, bo w nich kłamstwo, fałsz i obłuda się kryje.

Żyd, siewca nędzy, głodu i pomoru, oszukuje Cię i prowadzi na bezdroża pod płaszczykiem ponętnych wizyj, jakie Ci ukazuje.

Żyd — to nie obrońca Twój! To zdrajca, podżegacz walk bratobójczych i rewolucyj, które tylko jemu wychodzą na korzyść, a Tobie przynoszą głód, nędzę i niewolę. To szatan kusiciel w ludzkim ciele, który Cię chce powieść na zatracenie!

Robotniku i Chłopie Polski! Nie ufaj nigdy żydowi! Uciekaj od niego, jak od morowego powietrza i pracuj w zwartym szeregu wraz z twymi Rodakami, którzy nie chcą dopuścić, by z Polski uczyniono kaźń sowiecką na wzór rosyjskiej i hiszpańskiej, a Ciebie zamieniono na bydlę robocze, pracujące od świtu do nocy o chłodzie i głodzie na rzecz pana Twego — żyda!

Robotniku i Chłopie Polski!

Ostrzegamy Cię przed żydem póki jeszcze czas! Ostrzegamy i wołamy: Bacz! Byś sam sobie, jak tylu innych, nie ukręcił powroza na szyję! Unikaj więc żyda!!!

Nakładem „Samoobrony Narodu" Poznań   Druk. Marcin Załachowski, Poznań 5

25

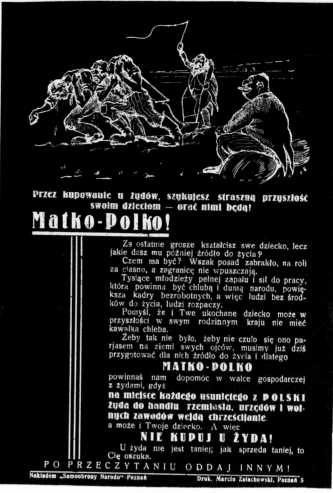

Przez kupowanie u żydów, szykujesz straszną przyszłość swoim dzieciom — orać nimi będą!

Matko-Polko!

Za ostatnie grosze kształcisz swe dziecko, lecz jakie dasz mu później źródło do życia?

Czem ma być? Wszak posad zabrakło, na roli za ciasno, a zagranicę nie wpuszczają.

Tysiące młodzieży pełnej zapału i sił do pracy, która powinna być chlubą i dumą narodu, powiększa kadry bezrobotnych, a więc ludzi bez środków do życia, ludzi rozpaczy.

Pomyśl, że i Twe ukochane dziecko może w przyszłości w swym rodzinnym kraju nie mieć kawałka chleba.

Żeby tak nie było, żeby nie czuło się ono parjasem na ziemi swych ojców, musimy już dziś przygotować dla nich źródło do życia i dlatego

MATKO-POLKO

powinnaś nam dopomóc w walce gospodarczej z żydami, gdyż

na miejsce każdego usuniętego z POLSKI żyda do handlu, rzemiosła, urzędów i wolnych zawodów wejdą chrześcijanie.

a może i Twoje dziecko. A więc

NIE KUPUJ U ŻYDA!

U żyda nie jest taniej; jak sprzeda taniej, to Cię oszuka.

PO PRZECZYTANIU ODDAJ INNYM!

Nakładem „Samoobrony Narodu"·Poznań   Druk. Marcin Załachowski, Poznań 5

2

RODACY!

Giną nasi synowie z rąk żydowskich, a my żydów popieramy. Nosimy im pieniądze na walkę z nami.

Czyż to nie wstyd i hańba!

Zbudź się sumienie polskie!

Niechaj niewinna krew pomordowanych naszych współbraci stanie Wam przed oczyma, kiedy macie popełnić czyn, wołający o pomstę do Boga, niosąc pieniądze żydowi.

Opamiętaj się Rodaku i Ty Matko-Polko!
Unikaj swego wroga-żyda!

Popieraj tylko swoich!

Nakładem „Samoobrony Narodu" Poznań   Druk. Marcin Załachowski, Poznań 5

27

Pamiętaj, że żyd Cię zawsze okradnie!

28

(25–28) Pre-war antisemitic Polish electoral leaflets and a popular postcard.

Warschau, 12.Juli
Die Eisenbahndirektion in Kattowitz hat, da sich die Juden wiederholt über das abweisende Verhalten der übrigen Fahrgäste beklagten, auf einer Hauptstrecke besondere Abteile eingeführt.
Die jüdische Presse ist über diese Lösung des Problems "entrüstet" und beklagt sich darüber, dass die Eisenbahnbeamten jüdische Passagiere, die in andere Abteile einstiegen, mit Gewalt in die für sie bestimmten Sonderabteile beförderten.

32

30

31

29

(29) Illustrated signboard on a Polish store in Mlawa (Poland) calling for an anti-Jewish boycott, 1922. (30) A Polish legionnaire cuts the beard of a Jew in a scene of a theatrical presentation in Vilna. (31) The house of Polish academicians in Vilna, decorated with slogans calling for separate Jewish seats at the universities. (32) German-Polish newspaper shows a cartoon depicting a train with special carriages for dogs and for Jews.

KOVOKINC
ŽU
ŽYDIŠKU
gaĺvaĺu:

Žīdu loma cilvēces vēsturē.

Vecā derība. Talmūds. Brīvmūrnieki jeb masoni. Ciānas gudro protokoli. Rituālas slepkavibas u. c.

ŪKININKAI !
NEPIRKITE
PAS ŽYDUS
NIEKO.

35

34

„Tautas Vairoga" Izdevn., Rīgā, Daugavgrīvas ielā 18, dz. 5.

36

33

(33) "Down with the Jewish Terror." A flier tha supposedly circulated in Moscow and Kiev 1936. (34–35) Two handwritten anti-Jewis fliers, Ponevezh (Lithuania), 1939. (36) Cove of an antisemitic pamphlet with the Naz emblem, published in Riga (Latvia), 1934.

39

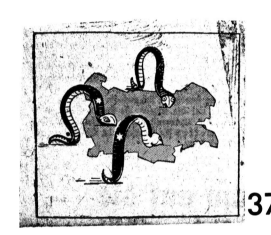

37

38

40

42

(37) Bulgarian anti-Jewish flier, reproduced by *Das 12 Uhr Blatt* (Berlin), January 2, 1939. **(38–39)** Two antisemitic posters in pre-war Rumania. **(40)** "Hungarian Christmas 1937." Hungarians must shovel the snow in front of a bar to make way for a Jewish couple arriving by car. **(41)** A 1907 Croatian antisemitic satirical publication; used in a 1942 book by E. Bauer. **(42)** Antisemitic cartoon in the Greek journal *Makedonia*, May 1933.

Christian

Vigilantes

Arise!

BUY

GENTILE

EMPLOY

GENTILE

VOTE

GENTILE

Boycott the Movies!

HOLLYWOOD is the Sodom and Gomorrha

WHERE

INTERNATIONAL JEWRY

CONTROLS

VICE - DOPE - GAMBLING

where

YOUNG GENTILE GIRLS ARE RAPED

by

JEWISH PRODUCERS, DIRECTORS, CASTING DIRECTORS

WHO GO UNPUNISHED

THE JEWISH HOLLYWOOD ANTI-NAZI LEAGUE CONTROLS

COMMUNISM

IN THE MOTION PICTURE INDUSTRY

STARS, WRITERS AND ARTISTS ARE COMPELLED TO PAY FOR COMMUNISTIC

ACTIVITIES

43

A Carnegie Institution Genealogy

ROOSEVELT'S JEWISH ANCESTRY

"HE IS NOT ONE OF US!"

(Reprint from Oct. 15, 1936, issue of "The Revealer," of Wichita, Kan., Rev. G. B. Winrod, Editor.)

The chart shown below, prepared by the Carnegie Institution of Washington, D. C., has come as a shocking revelation to millions of American citizens. It explains things in connection with Roosevelt's Administration which can not otherwise be understood.

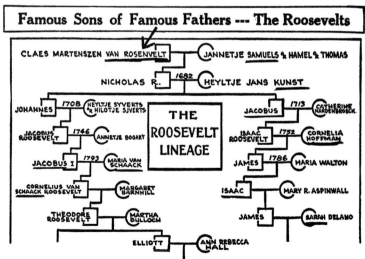

(43—44) Anti-Jewish fliers, United States, 1930s.

44

THE PLUNDERERS UNION

TROJAN HORSE - FIFTH COLUMN

45

Jesus Christ - Martin Luther - Mohammed - P o p e
Clement VIII - Benjamin Franklin - Ulysses Grant
James A. Garfield - and Henry Ford unite with 50 other
famous personages in saying:

JEWS
are TRAITORS to America
and should not be trusted.
Buy Gentile

46

Onward Jewish Soldiers!

47

(45–47) Antisemitic fliers in the United States,
1930s.

49

48

(48) Antisemitic flier in the United States, 1930s. (49) This American antisemitic flier of 1909 and 1913 was reprinted in the *Rostocker Anzeiger* of April 25, 1939 and in many other German newspapers.

Le PATRIOTE

Journal hebdomadaire paraissant le jeudi — 5 SOUS — Rédigé en collaboration

VOL. I — No 40 — MONTREAL, 2 FEVRIER 1934 — 1725, rue Saint-Denis, Montréal

La race d'Israël est la plus dégénérée du monde

Révélation écrasantes des statistiques officielles et des grands savants. — La démence précoce, la démence périodique, l'idiotie, l'imbécillité, la dégénérescence héréditaire atteignent chez les Juifs des chiffres hors de toute proportion. — Affaissement affreux de la morale. — Textes de médecins mondialement connus. — Les auteurs non-juifs. — Péril très grave dont les races saines doivent se garer. — La "race-élue", la race supérieure ne l'est que dans la décomposition et la dépravation.

LES COUCHES SUPERIEURES JUIVES SONT LES PLUS FORTEMENT ATTEINTES

La race juive est, à plusieurs points de vue, un danger constant pour les races au milieu desquelles elle se développe. Danger spirituel d'abord, parce qu'au sein des sociétés chrétiennes elle fait oeuvre d'anti-christianisme; danger moral parce qu'au sein des races occidentales elle entretient un foyer de contamination par les moeurs orientales les plus dépravées; danger économique, parce qu'elle s'est spécialisée dans le parasitisme et l'absorption des richesses matérielles par le moyens les plus abjects et les plus dépourvus de scrupule; danger social et hygiénique parce qu'elle est la plus dégénérée, physiquement et mentalement. Il suffit, à ce dernier point de vue, de consulter les autorités médicales, juives et non-juives, pour en trouver la preuve indiscutable.

Le célèbre médecin juif HANS ULLMANN, dans "Archive fuer Rassen und Gesellschafts Biologie", donne pour l'Allemagne les statistiques suivantes des proportions de chrétiens et Juifs internés dans les hôpitaux d'aliénés en Allemagne, chiffres confirmés par "Preussische Statistik", XXX, 7, et Konfessionstatistik eberda", p. 80-81 :

Année	Chrétiens	Juifs
1871	22	28
1881	29.7	92.2
1890	39.7	120.4
1895	58	145.6
1900	63.3	163.1

Et les statistiques allemandes, que l'on est à compiler pour les années qui suivent, accusent une progression plus grande encore, affirme-t-on.

En Italie, dans la "Revue critique de clinique médicale", le DR SILVAGNI, donnant des statistiques semblables à celles de l'Allemagne, écrit :

"A l'immunité que montrent les Juifs par rapport aux grandes épidémies populaires correspond le fait qu'ils sont spécialement sujets à d'autres maladies, par exemple les maladies du système nerveux et du cerveau".

Aux Etats-Unis, le docteur juif MAURICE FISHBURG écrit ; dans "Eugenic Factors in Jewish Life":

"Les Juifs ont un nombre disproportionné de faibles d'esprit, d'idiots et d'imbéciles. C'est un fait notoire que les Juifs ont un fort pourcentage des neurasthéniques et des névroses. En Europe, la cécité, la surdité, le mutisme, l'idiotie et l'insanité sont de deux à cinq fois plus fréquentes chez les Juifs que chez les Gentils".

Dans "Zeitschrift fuer Sozialwissenschaft", 12ème année, 1909, p. 663, le célèbre médecin juif RUDOLF WASSERMANN écrit :

"Nous possédons, en chiffres, un matériel copieux qui montre que les Juifs, tout particulièrement, sont sujets aux maladies cérébrales et dans la doctrine spécialiste, il y a unanimité pour le reconnaître". Et il ajoute des tableaux statistiques en preuve de son affirmation.

Pour la Russie, le DR RAJASANSKI, dans "Aertl Zeitschrift", 1920, souligne particulièrement la disposition des Juifs-russes pour les maladies mentales.

(Suite à la page 6)

L'unité nationale sera possible par le PARTI NATIONAL SOCIAL CHRETIEN

"VISA LE NOIR, TUA LE BLANC"

Le bill David contre les "agitateurs".

Nos ministres de Québec se grattent la tête et se tordent la moustache afin de tordre le cou à ceux qu'ils considèrent comme communistes. Ils ont fait adopter une législation l'année dernière pour arrêter les agissements d'Albert Saint-Martin et de son école. Il est vrai que Saint-Martin prêchait l'anticléricalisme, l'abolition de nos institutions religieuses et de notre système capitaliste, au su et au vu de tout le monde, en plein Palais de Justice, ou en plein Champ de Mars, depuis vingt-cinq ans quand on s'est aperçu qu'il pouvait faire du mal. On savait pourtant, auparavant, passé à Québec toutes sortes de législations draconiennes: loi Roberts, restrictions des clauses de la loi du libelle, loi du libelle radiophonique, bill philosémite contre le "Miroir" et le "Goglu", etc.

Malgré la loi de l'année dernière destinée à tuer l'Université ouvrière de Saint-Martin, ses disciples continuent leurs cours de démolition sociale, sous divers noms, et la police Jargailles paraît être impuissante à les mâter.

Cette année, M. David proposera paraît-il, un nouveau bill par lequel les chefs de police devront approuver, au préalable, toutes les circulaires convoquant des assemblées. On espère par là empêcher les "agitateurs" de rassembler des auditeurs.

Mais comment les chefs de police, ou leurs substituts (le plus souvent obtus) pourront-ils découvrir une convocation communiste dans les termes d'une simple annonce ? Ces "coquins" leur joueront certainement "des tours", comme dit la chanson.

En attendant la rédaction définitive du Bill David, mettons-nous en garde contre la vague du bill.

Quel sens veut-on donner au mot "agitateurs" ?

Sont-ce les gens qui critiquent le pouvoir ?

Sont-ce les fascistes ?

Sont-ce les "Jeune-Canada" ?

Avec un texte de loi aussi vague on pourra arrêter n'importe quel orateur "bona fide" et empêcher des tenues d'une assemblée contre le Juifs ou contre les trusts, par exemple.

Que M. David n'aille pas renouveler l'aventure du chasseur de la chanson :

"Visa le noir, tua le blanc".

Le premier article du programme du Parti, qui apporte une formule nouvelle et définitive à la question nationale, sera expliqué par M. Adrien Arcand, le 22 février prochain, au grand ralliement du Monument National. — Autres questions capitales qui seront discutées, en regard des revendications du Parti de la renaissance canadienne. — Les billets s'enlèvent rapidement. — Evénement qui restera mémorable.

Tout fait prévoir qu'il y aura une foule considérable, au Monument National, le 22 février prochain, lorsque le programme du Parti National Social Chrétien sera exposé pour la première fois. Les billets s'enlèvent plus rapidement que pour tout autre ralliement précédent. Les fervents du mouvement ne se contentent pas de réserver des sièges pour eux-mêmes, ils en prennent aussi pour leurs amis et ceux qu'ils croient que cette soirée intéressera. L'élément féminin, qui a à se prononcer sur les questions nationales, semble devoir être bien représenté.

Pourquoi n'avons-nous jamais eu d'unité nationale, sous aucun régime, pourquoi met-on même en doute la valeur de la Confédération canadienne, qu'est-ce qui doit être fait pour parvenir à l'unité nationale, sans rien sacrifier de nos caractéristiques ethniques ? Voilà des questions d'une extrême importance qui font l'objet du premier article du Parti National Social Chrétien, et que M. Adrien Arcand développera, au grand ralliement du 22 février.

Mais la question nationale n'est pas la seule qu'embrasse le programme du Parti National Social Chrétien. Il y a aussi la question impériale, qui existe, que l'on a toujours embrouillée mais qu'il faut définir clairement une fois pour toutes, afin de n'avoir qu'une seule mentalité nationale à son sujet; il y a aussi la question sociale, qu'il est urgent de régler dans le meilleur sens, si l'on veut éviter qu'elle soit réglée dans un sens anti-canadien et anti-chrétien; il y a la question économique, qui doit être restaurée de façon à empêcher dans l'avenir les injustices, les exploitations, les abus, les désorganisations dont la population a eu toujours à souffrir sous la démocratie; il y a la question financière, qui doit prendre un aspect nouveau, tout en tenant compte des progrès et des besoins modernes. Toutes ces questions font l'objet d'articles clairs, précis et catégoriques, dans le programme du Parti National Social Chrétien. De même sont clairs et catégoriques les articles du programme qui concernent les réformes parlementaires, gouvernementales, agricoles, etc., que réclame le Parti des temps nouveaux, le Parti de l'avenir, le Parti de la renaissance canadienne.

Le programme du Parti National Social Chrétien sera toute une révélation pour ceux qui attendaient un cri d'espoir et de confiance, en ces temps troublés, ce sera une vive satisfaction pour tous les esprits inquiets qui se demandaient si rien ne serait fait pour conjurer le grand péril qui bouleverse le monde et menace notre beau pays.

Les billets sont en vente, aux prix de 10, 25 et 50 sous (loges, $1.), aux bureaux du "Patriote", 1725, rue Saint-Denis, HArbour 8216. Les Juifs ne sont pas admis à cette soirée, pas plus que dans les rangs du Parti. (Les commandes par téléphone sont remplies sur paiement).

50

The Jewish Problem in South Africa

51

(50) Canadian antisemitic weekly, 1934. **(51)** Cover of a South African antisemitic pamphlet, 1937. **(52–53)** Antisemitic cartoons in *Clarinada* (Argentina), 1930s.

53

52

54

55

56

II. THE JEWS ARE OUR MISFORTUNE

(54) Julius Streicher speaking at a street meeting against Jews. **(55)** Posters announcing an antisemitic meeting in Nuremberg with the participation of Hitler and Streicher, 1920s. **(56)** Antisemitic emblem of the *Stürmer* publishing house.

HETZE IM BILD...

Selbst die Ritualmordlüge wird noch

- leider erfolgreich - propagiert

(57) A montage of Nazi propaganda against Jews prior to the advent of the Third Reich; from a pamphlet published by the Central Verein deutscher Statsburger jüdischen Glaubens.

(58–59) Two issues of the Stürmer, published by Julius Streicher, 1934 and 1936.

Deutsche Frauen und Mädchen
die Juden sind Euer Verderben

Vor zweitausend Jahren habe ich die Juden als Teufelsvolk
verflucht, und Ihr macht ein Gottesvolk aus ihnen

Nicht Haß anderen Völkern, sondern Liebe zu der deutschen Nation!
(Rede des Führers: 24. 10. 1933)

Wer dem Juden vertraut
geht erbarmungslos zu Grunde

Die Völker nicht, der Jude will den Krieg
Die Völker bluten um des Juden Sieg

Würde man die Menschheit in drei Arten teilen, in Kulturbegründer, Kulturträger und Kulturzerstörer, dann käme als Vertreter der ersten wohl nur der
Arier in Frage. (Adolf Hitler: „Mein Kampf")

Der Stürmer
ist der treue Wächter des deutschen Volkes

Es hat der Teufel viele schon bestochen - Auf seinen Leim ist klein
und Groß gekrochen - Er macht auch nicht vor Klostermauern halt -
Denn wer ihn nicht durchschaut, verfällt ihm allzubald

Alles was groß, hoch und heilig war, hat der Jude in den Staub gerissen
(Rede des Führers: 21. 8. 1924)

Der Stürmer
schützt Dich vor jüdischer Ausbeutung

Was willste mit ä Katz. Fang mer die Ratten mit der Falle und
machen Hackfleisch davon. Der Goi frißt alles, wenn es nur billig ist.

Der Jude wird immer und ewig der geborene Privatkapitalist allerschlimmster
ausbeuterischster Art sein. (Rede des Führers: 28. 7. 1922)

Der Stürmer leuchtet hinein
in die Geheimnisse des Judentums

Gott der Gerechte, laß uns finden ä Fleckchen auf der Welt
wo ka Mensch liest den Stürmer

Der Jude ist kein Herrenvolk, er ist ein Ausbeuterer, ein Räubervolk
(Rede des Führers: 28. 7. 1922)

SA und Stürmer
marschieren und kämpfen gemeinsam

Unser Ziel: Was der Führer will,
Unser Streben: Deutschland muß leben,
Die Losung sei: Von Jud und Judenknechten frei

Wir haben das Land durch Kampf erobert, jetzt müssen wir es durch
Frieden bestellen. (Rede des Führers: 12. 7. 1933)

Ohne
Lösung der Judenfrage

keine Erlösung des
deutschen Volkes!

(60) Illustrations to anti-Jewish slogans by A. Hitler,
booklet published by Streicher's *Der Stürmer*. The title
page consists of Streicher's slogan: "Without solution
of the Jewish problem there can be no salvation of the
German People."

61

65

Ein feiner Schnappfchuß
Jude und Jüdin blicken entfeßt auf einen
Stürmer-Aushang

Ein Jude, angetan mit voller Fluchgebets-
ausrüftung. Im Hintergrund ein Stürmer-
kaften.

64

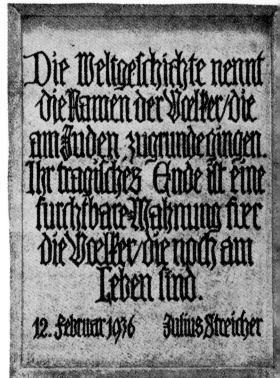

62

63

The *Stürmer* and anti-Jewish slogans were displayed
on the streets and in other public places. **(61)** The
Stürmer displayed beside the Jewish community house
of Halberstadt. **(62)** An anti-Jewish panel put up by
Streicher in Rothenburg ob der Tauber on February
12, 1936. **(63–64)** Jews were forced to be photo-
graphed in front of displayed copies of the *Stürmer*.
(65) "Judaism is Criminalism—Read the extra edition
of the *Stürmer*"; sign displayed at the Schönbrunn
Palace in Vienna.

N.S.B.O. Rh. West　　　Bahn-Betriebswerk.

Ohne Lösung der Judenfrage —— Keine Erlösung des deutschen Volkes

66

67

68

69

(66–69) Antisemitic newspapers and signs displayed in public places.

71

Stürmer-Kasten

„Ob es regnet, stürmt oder schneit,
der Stürmer kommt zu jeder Zeit."
So schreibt uns der Stürmerverkäufer Ewert
aus Osterode/Ostpr.

72

70

(70–73) Reading and selling the *Stürmer* and the *Judenkenner*.

73

76

75

Kolosseum

spricht am Freitag, den 2. November 1928, abends 8 Uhr
unser Führer

Hitler

über

Rasse und Zukunft!

Mitwirkung der S.-A.-Kapelle und des Spielmannszuges Franken.
Saalöffnung nicht vor ½7 Uhr. Eintritt 50 Pfg.
Erwerbslose Parteigenossen gegen Ausweis 20 Pfg.
Juden haben keinen Zutritt!

Nationalsozialistische Deutsche Arbeiter-Partei
Ortsgruppe Nürnberg

74

III. RACISM

(74) Poster announcing a meeting with Hitler's speech on "Race and Future," Nuremberg, November 2, 1928. "Jews are not admitted." **(75–76)** German women and Jews being paraded through streets for having had sexual relations.

80

77

78

79

(77) A Jew being paraded with the sign, "I raped a Christian girl." **(78)** A postcard containing a threat to brand with acid the faces of German women who keep company with Jews or supposed Jews, 1933. **(79)** Warnings to German women displayed at a Nazi meeting against Jewish rapists, 1935. **(80)** Comparison between a German woman and a Jewish woman in a book by R. Körber, 1939.

Der jüdische „Brotherr" —
Leibeigenschaft im 20. Jahrhundert.

Talmud: (Rabbi Abarbanel)
Das Weib des Fremden, das nicht eine Jüdin ist, ist nur ein Vieh".

Jüdischer Mädchenhandel
Der Mädchenhandel ist restlos in den Händen der Juden.
Die jüdische Zeitung „The Jewish Chronicle" (Die jüdische Chronik) schreibt selbst:

(81) Illustrations from Dr. Kurt Plischke's book, The Jew as a Seducer.

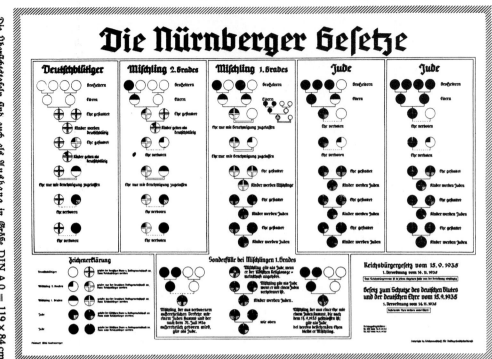

83

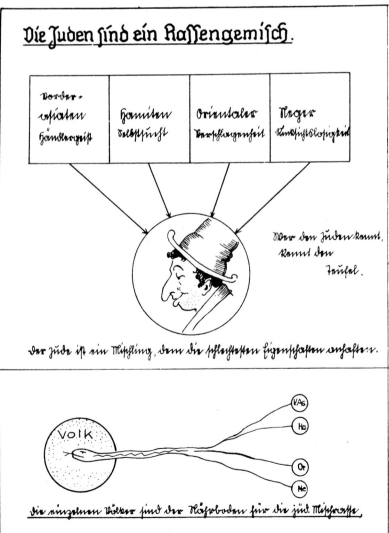

84

(82) One of many Nazi commentaries on the Nuremberg racial laws. **(83–84)** Tables explaining the Nuremberg racial laws.

82

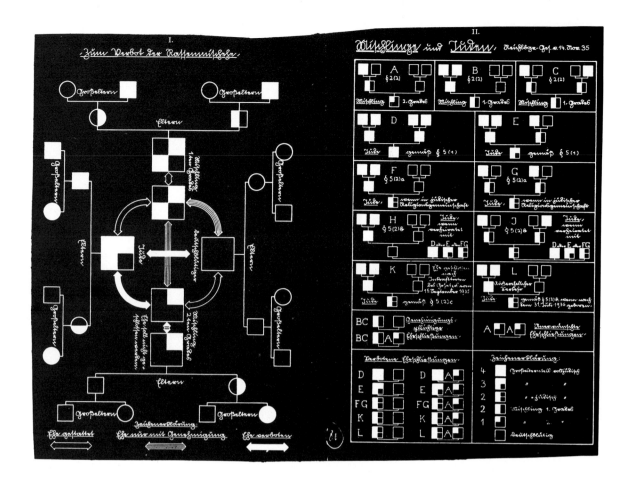

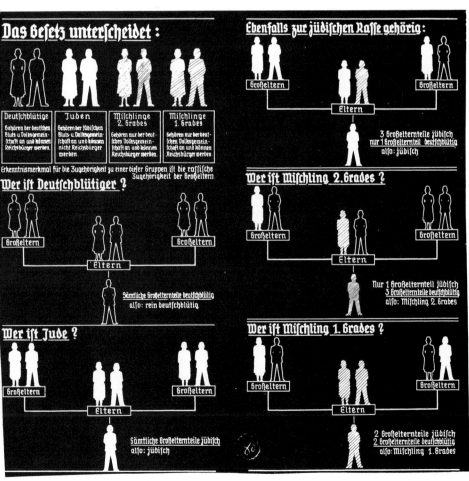

85

(85–86) Tables explaining the Nuremberg racial law in books by M. Eichler and Dr. W. Dittrich.

Erstes Rasse-Amt! Gewerkschafts-Korruption

„Reichsstand des deutschen Handels"
Heute Vereinheitlichung des Einzelhandels erfolgt!

87

88

89

(87) The *Acht Uhr-Abendblatt* of May 4, 1933, reported on the opening of the first office for race problems in Dortmund. (88–89) The Nuremberg racist law reported in the German press.

Keine Rasse, sondern ein Rassengemisch!

In eindrucksvoller Weise bestätigt dieses Bild eines jungen
Mädchens, daß in den Adern der Juden Negerblut fließt

Der Stürmer
Hauptschriftleitung

91

Deutsche **Volksgesundheit**

auf Blut und Boden!

Die „Deutsche Volksgesundheit" ist unter neuer Führung und
in neuer Ausgestaltung wieder erschienen. Sie wird herausgegeben
von Julius Streicher.

Sie kämpft für die natürliche Heilweise und macht Front
gegen jüdischen Geist und Einfluß in der Medizin

Aus dem Inhalt der 1. Februarnummer:

Die Folgen der Rassenschande
Artfremdes Blut wirkt wie Gift
Emil Schlegel, der Volksarzt ohne Doktortitel
Englische Ärzte über Tierversuche
Güsse als Hausmittel
Vor einem Heilpraktikergesetz
Briefe an eine werdende Mutter
Mein Kind will nicht essen
u. a. m.

Bestellung beim Berl. „Deutsche Volksgesundheit", Nürnberg-A,
oder bei jeder Postanstalt zum Preise von monatlich 60 Pfg.

90

93

Weiß und schwarz.

Die jüdische Schlange sagt es immer wieder, alle Menschen seien
gleich! Damit sich die Nichtjuden an die Rassenschande gewöhnen
veröffentlichen jüdische Zeitungen in Amerika immer wieder Bil
der, die verschiedenfarbige Menschen in trautem Zusammensein
zeigen.

92

(90) Flier of *Deutsche Volksgesundheit,* published by
Julius Streicher, to fight against the "Jewish spirit and
influence in medicine." **(91–93)** Racist propaganda
against Jews and Negroes in the United States,
prepared by the *Stürmer*.

German Racial and Population Questions in their World Significance.

By W. Gross, M.D. Head of the Racio-Political Department, Berlin.

Among the many problems which we have tackled in the New Germany the population question is the one that has been least understood. Today however we find that others beyond our borders are also beginning to realize the seriousness of the population and racio-political questions. The opinion has been held abroad that our efforts to raise the birth rate were leading to a forcible expansion of our vital national energy as well as to political tension on our frontiers. In reality the reason for our efforts to increase the population is our great uneasiness that today we are already registering a drop in population figures. The German birth rate has for years past been insufficient to maintain the population at its minimum level. The birth rate in 1933 had dropped to such a low level that, if it were maintained, the German nation at the end of the present century would have diminished to less than 47 million inhabitants.

A question of domestic principle.

Our main efforts are not directed towards measures of economic impulse but rather primarily towards domestic conduct. A sound and healthy nation will always be blessed with the requisite number of children. In the final analysis the bringing of children into the world is a question of education based on a definite Weltanschauung. We have, therefore, concentrated very strongly on education and upbringing and have discussed these questions very freely and frankly in public. We do so because we see in our appeal to a healthy instinct the most suitable weapon for assisting us in our fight on this population question. We believe that a healthy nation imbued with self-confidence, will sooner or later recover that healthy instinct which will in every healthy family quite naturally lead to a desire for children.

The success of the German population policy.

The success of the German population policy is not yet such that the danger of a further depopulation has been averted. Nevertheless, in 1934/35 we experienced an increase in population when compared with 1933, this increase amounting to approximately 25%. This, in the course of twelve months is a great success. But it is wrong to believe that the danger of a decline in the birth rate has now been overcome. Statistics show that an increase in the birth rate of 25% is insufficient to permanently maintain the population of the Third Reich.

It is wrong for people abroad to believe that the increase in the German birth rate means a corresponding increase in the number of inhabitants as well as, sooner or later, to a pressure for expansion into neighbouring countries. The fact is that we shall have our hands full up to the end of this century if we are to maintain our birth rate and our population.

Racial culture and population policy.

Eugenics, recognized today throughout the world as a science, is confronted with the question as to whether it is not possible to increase population in the one or other human group and remove all symptoms of degeneration among nations. A symptom of degeneration is the fact that among civilized nations in particular we find innumerable people who, dependent upon their own energy, are not capable of existence. Their lack of vital energy is not due to any ailment or accident but is purely a case of hereditary affliction.

The laws of heredity.

There is a difference between people who lose their mental faculties through damage to their skulls and those who are born with a diseased brain. In the former case there does exist a hope of recovery and what is more important, the trouble is limited to the person concerned. But there are in existence a whole series of ailments not brought on by accident or infection but which have been introduced in this world at birth through heredity. A weak-minded or mentally deficient child, mentally deficient not through any accidental skull trouble—but because its condition is hereditary—is incapable of being cured either by medical skill or the kind attention of its teachers at school. And the descendants of such children will in their turn be similarly afflicted with the same hereditary ailment. All this is an indisputable fact which only the genealogical tables of the families in question reveal to us.

Precautionary measures against degeneration.

If we are desirous of taking up the fight against hereditary disease we can only do so by seeing to it that the propagation of further progeny is made impossible, that is, we must see to it that these people discontinue having further children. And here we have at our disposal only one really humane method. This is the process of sterilization which we in Germany have selected for the prevention of hereditary disease. This method has for a long time been recognized and legally adopted in a large number of states belonging to the American Union, in certain cantons in Switzerland and in other countries as well.

In the case of the weak-minded and mentally deficient, we are unable to teach them to be sensible and decline to have children. Therefore they simply must be relieved of this responsibility. And this is only possible by means of sterilization. We have firmly declined to adopt any other measure such as permanently isolating these poor unfortunates for we regard this as inhuman and unworthy. The better way is to sterilize these people by means of a small and harmless operation and as far as possible give them their freedom.

It is an act of gross and deliberate neglect for intelligent people to stand by helpless—fully conscious of the misery and suffering to come—and be witness to the propagation of children who can only be a burden to themselves and others. One should pay a visit to a modern home sheltering between 800 and 1000 of these unfortunate imbeciles. It is appalling and heartrending to see their misery, their suffering and their animal instincts. They are people whom we are unable to help for the rest of their lives.

Germany is convinced that the prevention of hereditary diseased offspring is a moral task. We are also convinced that there are no moral or religious reasons for opposing the truth and the necessity for this measure. We assume that the results of such preventative measures will be welcomed as desirable by all honest people, for they accord with the principles of charity, morality and humanity.

Long-range political policy.

The results of the measures for the prevention of hereditary diseased offspring will naturally only be noticeable in years to come in that no further mentally diseased children will be born. In about thirty years time Germany will have removed a load of affliction under which other countries are today heavily labouring.

All persons who are the victims of hereditary disease are a charge on public funds. Everywhere special homes have to be built to shelter these poor unfortunates for they lack the vital energy necessary for self-support. In Germany the annual expenditure involved for the care and support of these people has reached a figure over 2 Milliard Reichsmarks. This huge sum will cease to be spent when, as previously stated, in thirty years time the number of afflicted people has been considerably reduced by death and when additional cases are no longer being born.

The application of the German Law of Sterilization.

The application of the sterilization law in Germany has been carried out very smoothly. A marked feature has been the number of cases of people who, realizing their condition,

No. 982. Engl.

(94) English leaflet praising the German racist policies, published by the Fichte Association (Fichte-Bund) of Hamburg.

95

96

(95–96) Tables explaining the racist theories being shown at a "scientific" conference held in Paris during the German occupation.

Fortränn

Franz Wilhelm

*1821 in: Prag 475 — II.

in:

Fortränn Valentin

Anna geb. Ackermann

m. Kath. des 8: röm. Kath. der 9: röm. Kath

. Stephan in Prag — 3917/XIV
324

Die Richtigkeit dieser Eintragung wird — auf Grund vorgelegter Urkunde — bescheinigt.
18. 3. 43.
Worte gestrichen hinzugefügt

Kirchbf., Standesb., Notar

in:

Die Richtigkeit dieser Eintragung wird — auf Grund vorgelegter Urkunde — bescheinigt.
Worte gestrichen hinzugefügt

Siegel

Bekenntnis:

Bekenntnis:

Kirchbf., Standesb., Notar

⑤ Geburtsname: Neumann
(Mutter von 2)

Vornamen: Anna Barbara

ist geboren am: 15. 8. 1834 in: Obecnitz
getauft am: 16. 8. 1834 in: Obecnitz

als Tochter des [10]: Neumann Josef

und der (11): Anna geb. Lang

Bekenntnis der 5: röm. Kath. des 10: röm. Kath. der 11 röm. Kath

beurkundet beim
Standesamt: Pibrans

Register-Nr.:
2640/19/104

Kath. Pfarramt:

Die Richtigkeit dieser Eintragung wird — auf Grund vorgelegter Urkunde — bescheinigt.
18. 3. 43
Worte gestrichen hinzug

Kirchbf., Standesb., N

Sie ist gestorben am: in:

beurkundet beim
Standesamt/Pfarramt:

Register-Nr.:

Die Richtigkeit dieser Eintragung wird — auf Grund vorgelegter Urkunde — bescheinigt.
Worte gestrichen hinzug

Siegel

Bekenntnis:

Kirchbf., Standesb., N

Die Ehe von ④ ∞ ⑤ wurde geschlossen:

am: 11. X. 1853 in: Dobryschütz

beurkundet beim
Stadtesamt/Pfarramt: Dobryschütz Register-Nr.: X/12

Die Richtigkeit dieser Eintragung wird — auf Grund vorgelegter Urkunde — bescheinigt.
18. 3. 43
Worte gestrichen hinzugefügt

Kirchbf., Standesb., Notar

② Name: Vordren
(Vater von 1)

Vornamen: Wilhelm Josef Bekenntnis: röm. Kath.

ist geboren am: 14. 3. 1854 in: Stekna
getauft am: 15. 3. 1854 in: Stekna als Sohn von 4 und 5. Beurkundet beim

Standesamt: Register-Nr.: 9/91/115 beim Kath. Pfarramt: Steknitz

Er ist gestorben am: 5. 10. 1926 in: Wlaschim

als (Beruf): Fürst Auersperg'scher Revierförster i. R.

Beurkundet beim
Standesamt/Pfarramt: Wlaschim Register-Nr.: 341/VI.-11 Bekenntnis: röm. Kath.

Die Richtigkeit dieser Eintragung wird — auf Grund vorgelegter Urkunde — bescheinigt.
20.11.42
Worte gestrichen hinzugefügt

Deutscher Notar
Kirchbf., Standesb., Notar

Die Richtigkeit dieser Eintragung wird — auf Grund vorgelegter Urkunde — bescheinigt.
Worte gestrichen hinzugefügt

Siegel

Kirchbf., Standesb., Notar

Die Ehe von ② ∞ ③ wu

am: 8. 3. 1890 in: Wlasch

beurkundet beim Dekanal
Standesamt/Pfarramt: Wlaschim

① Name: Vordren

Vornamen: Josef Wilhelm

ist geboren am: 21.11.1890 in: Glazuta (= Karlshütter
getauft am: 7. 12. 1890 in: Görovice (= Masern)

Standesamt: Register-Nr.: 2/61

Er/Sie hat die Ehe geschlossen am: 26. 6. 1937 in:

Vornamen, Name, Beruf: Grete, geborene

beurkundet beim
Standesamt/Pfarramt: Prag Regis

(97) Certificate of Aryan descent issued to Josef Wilhelm Wordren of Prague, March 1943.

Name: (Vater von 5) Proch**á**ska

Karl

geboren am: 14.8.1829 in: Domaschin

getauft am: 15.8.1829 in: Domaschin

Sohn des [12]: Prochaska Johann

der (13): Anna geb. Poselt

Bekenntnis des 6: röm. Kath. des 12: röm. Kath. der 13: röm. Kath.

beurkundet beim Standesamt: Domaschin — Register-Nr.: 11.- VII /51

kath. Pfarramt:

Die Richtigkeit dieser Eintragung wird — auf Grund vorgelegter Urkunde — beicheinigt.
18. 3. 43.
Worte gestrichen hinzugefügt

Kirchbf., Standesb., Notar

ist gestorben am: in:

(Beruf):

beurkundet beim Landesamt/Pfarramt:

Register-Nr.: Bekenntnis:

Die Richtigkeit dieser Eintragung wird — auf Grund vorgelegter Urkunde — beicheinigt.
Worte gestrichen hinzugefügt
Siegel
Kirchbf., Standesb., Notar

---

(7) **Geburtsname:** Pik

Vornamen: Marie Karoline

ist geboren am: 6.2.1831 in: Wlaschim

getauft am: 6.2.1831 in: Wlaschim

als Tochter des (14): Pik Heinrich

und der (15): Marie geb. Harrer

Bekenntnis der 7: röm. Kath. des 14: röm. Kath. der 15: röm. Kath.

beurkundet beim Standesamt: Wlaschim — Register-Nr.: 1058

Kath. Pfarramt: VII - 118

Sie ist gestorben am: in:

beurkundet beim Standesamt/Pfarramt:

Register-Nr.: Bekenntnis:

Die Ehe von (6) ∞ (7) wurde geschlossen:

am: 22.10.1861 in: Wlaschim

beurkundet beim kath. Standesamt/Pfarramt: Wlaschim Register-Nr.: 939 - IV /21

Die Richtigkeit dieser Eintragung wird — auf Grund vorgelegter Urkunde — bescheinigt.
20.11.42
Worte gestrichen hinzugefügt
Siegel
Deutscher Notar
Kirchbf., Standesb., Notar

---

(3) **Geburtsname:** Prochazka

Vornamen: Franziska Elisabeth Bekenntnis: röm. Kath.

ist geboren am: 16.1. 1864 in: Wlaschim als Tochter von 6 und 7. Beurkundet beim

getauft am: 17.1. 1864 in: Wlaschim kath. Pfarramt: Wlaschim

Standesamt: Register-Nr.: St. XI /82 beim

Sie ist gestorben am: 1929 in: Woken bei Niemes

beurkundet beim Standesamt/Pfarramt:

Register-Nr.: Bekenntnis:

Die Richtigkeit dieser Eintragung wird — auf Grund vorgelegter Urkunde — bescheinigt.
20.11.42
Worte gestrichen hinzugefügt
Siegel
Deutscher Notar
Kirchbf., Standesb., Notar

Bekenntnis: röm. Kath.

von 2 und 3. Beurkundet beim

Pfarramt: Grcarice mit:

Bekenntnis:

Die Richtigkeit dieser Eintragung wird — auf Grund vorgelegter Urkunde — bescheinigt.
20.11.42
Worte gestrichen hinzugefügt
Siegel
Deutscher Notar
Kirchbf., Standesb., Notar

355 - IV /212

IV. ANTISEMITISM IN EDUCATION

(98) Pages from Elvira Bauer's booklet for children, published in 1936 by the *Stürmer* (continued on the next two pages).

(98) Pages from Elvira Bauer's booklet for children

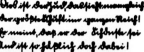

(98) Pages from Elvira Bauer's booklet for children

„Wenn ihr ein Kreuz seht, dann denkt an den grauenhaften Mord der Juden auf Golgatha ..."

„Der Gott des Juden ist das Geld. Und um Geld zu verdienen, begeht er die größten Verbrechen. Er ruht nicht eher, bis er auf einem großen Geldsack sitzen kann, bis er zum König des Geldes geworden ist."

„Hier, Kleiner, hast du etwas ganz Süßes! Aber dafür müßt ihr beide mit mir gehen ..."

Der Giftpilz

Ein Stürmerbuch für Jung u. Alt
Erzählungen von Ernst Hiemer
Bilder von Fips

Verlag Der Stürmer / Nürnberg

99

(99) Pages from *Der Giftpilz,* an antisemitic book for children by Ernst Hiemer, illustrated by Fips; published by the *Stürmer* in 1938.

Hinter den Brillengläsern funkeln zwei Verbrecheraugen und um die wulstigen Lippen spielt ein Grinsen.

„Wer gegen den Juden kämpft, ringt mit dem Teufel." Julius Streicher

„Die Judennase ist an ihrer Spitze gebogen. Sie sieht aus wie ein Sechser..."

„Am Bahnhof erwartete mich ein Mann. Er zog seinen Hut und war sehr freundlich zu mir. Aber ich merkte gleich, daß er ein Jude war..."

(99) Pages from *Der Giftpilz,* an antisemitic book for children by Ernst Hiemer, illustrated by Fips; published by the Stürmer in 1938.

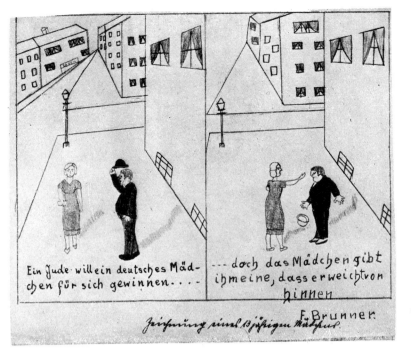

Ein Jude will ein deutsches Mädchen für sich gewinnen....

...doch das Mädchen gibt
ihm eine, dass er weicht von
hinnen

F. Brunner

101

14 jähriges jüdisches Mädchen

100

102

13 jähriges deutsches Mädchen

103

(100–103) Pages from Fritz Fink's book *Die Judenfrage in Unterricht* [The Jewish Question in Education], published in 1937 by the *Stürmer*. **(100)** The Aryan vs. the Jewish race. **(101)** The Jew tries to seduce a German girl; drawing by a thirteen-year-old German girl. **(102)** The poor Jew invaded Germany and leaves that country enriched for Palestine; drawing by a thirteen-year-old German child. **(103)** The Jew tries to ruin the peasant; drawing by a twelve-year-old German girl.

105

107

106

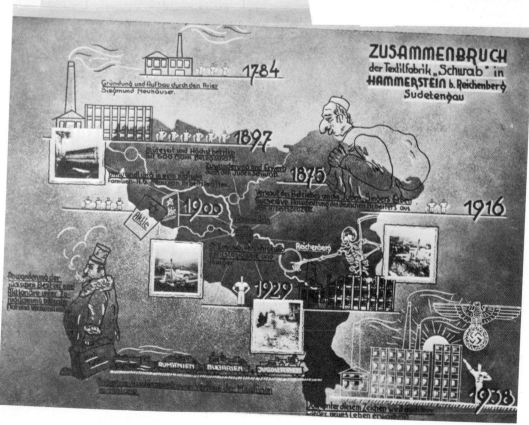

104

(104–106) Illustrations in the official Nazi handbook on education, *Erziehung . . . Ein Neur Weg:* (104) How Jews ruined a textile factory. (105) German theatre in Jewish hands. (106) Struggle against Jewish influence. (107) A child being shown how to paint the word "Jew" on a Jewish house.

109

110

108

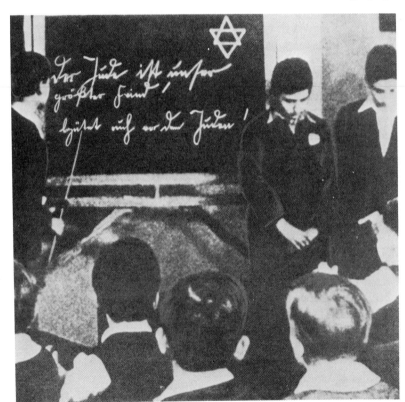

(108) Every Saturday the children of Schoenfeld (Baden) hanged a copy of the *Stürmer* on a maypole. (109) Burket, a teacher in Cologne, encourages children to study the Jewish question. On the blackboard is written: "Who knows the Jew knows the devil. No salvation for the German people without the solution of the Jewish question." (110) Jewish children being ridiculed in front of the class.

42

111

112

113

Hans Thoma „Deutsche Weisheit"

Ludwig Knaus „Salomonische Weishe

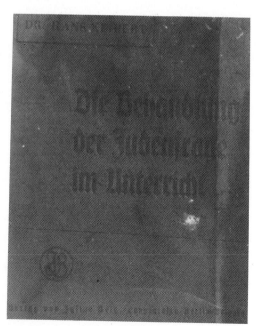

(111) Jews are excluded from schools, announces the *Völkischer Beobachter* of April 13, 1933. (112) The *Stürmer* of October 1936 contains a cartoon against the Bible, decorated with the Star of David and a cross, for the benefit of children. (113) Two illustrations used in *Kleines Juden-Brevier* to show the superiority of German education and the Aryan race, 1939. (114) H. Keipert's book on the Jewish question in education, 1940.

114

Henri Faugeras

Les Juifs
Peuple de Proie

LES DOCUMENTS CONTEMPORAINS

Dédié aux quarante millions de Français auxquels l'Enseignement public n'apprit jamais qu'une histoire écrite par des professeurs juifs.

115

— C'est bour mieux gourir, mon envant.

— Ma mère'grand, que vous avez de grandes oreilles!

— C'est bour mieux t'égouter, mon envant.

— Ma mère'grand, que vous avez un grand nez!

— C'est bour mieux renifler les bedides affaires ma ville.

— Ma mère'grand, que vous avez de gros yeux!

— C'est bour mieux te foir mon envant.

— Ma mère'grand, que vous avez de grandes dents!

— C'est bour mieux te groquer...

Et sur ces mots Grojuif s'élance sur Doulce France pour la dévorer. Mais elle recula épouvantée d'avoir eu confiance en un tel monstre : elle appela à l'aide.

Un des fils de la nouvelle France courut à son aide et arriva juste à temps pour délivrer Doulce France des doigts crochus de Grojuif.

Et dans l'azur, la « Vérité », de ses chauds rayons, put emplir le ciel de France pour se mêler à la clarté de la nouvelle Europe.

N.

116

(115) The jacket of a French antisemitic book deploring the use of books written by Jewish professors, 1943. (116) Pages from *Il était une fois,* French antisemitic book for children, 194—.

Debatte im Oberhaus

JÜDISCHE RUNDSCHAU

Einzelnummer 0,25 Goldmark

Erscheint jeden Dienstag, Freitag. Bezugspreis bei der Expedition monatlich 2.— Goldmark, vierteljährlich 5,75 Goldmark. Auslandsabonnements werden in der Währung der einzelnen Länder berechnet. Anzeigenpreis: 8 Gpf. Nonpareillezeile 0,50 G.-M. Stellengesuche 0,25 G.-M.

| Nummer 27 | Berlin, 4. IV. 1933 |

Redaktion, Verlag und Anzeigen-Verwaltung: Jüdische Rundschau G.m.b.H., Berlin W15, Meinekestr. 10. Telefon: J1 Bismarck 7165-70. Anzeigenschluß: Dienstag und Freitag nachmittags 4 Uhr. Redaktionsschluß Sonntag und Mittwoch nachmittag.

Postscheck-Konten: Berlin 173 92, Basel V 9355, Belgrad 680 32, Brüssel 394 33, Budapest 596 93, Danzig 1973, Haag 140 470, Prag 594 10, Riga 4155, Straßburg 164 30, Warschau 190 708, Wien 156 030. Bank-Konten: Dresdner Bank, Depositen-Kasse Berlin, Kurfürstendamm 52, Rumänische Kreditbank, Cernaui (Rumänien); Anglo Palestine Co. in Haifa, Jerusalem, Tel-Aviv.

XXXVIII. Jahrg.

Der Zionismus erstrebt für das jüdische Volk die Schaffung einer öffentlich-rechtlich gesicherten Heimstätte in Palästina. "Baseler Programm."

Tragt ihn mit Stolz, den gelben Fleck!

Der 1. April 1933 wird ein wichtiger Tag in der Geschichte der deutschen Juden, ja in der Geschichte des ganzen jüdischen Volkes bleiben. Die Ereignisse dieses Tages haben nicht nur eine politische und eine wirtschaftliche, sondern auch eine moralische und seelische Seite. Ueber die politischen und wirtschaftlichen Zusammenhänge ist in den Zeitungen viel gesprochen worden, wobei freilich häufig agitatorische Bedürfnisse die sachliche Erkenntnis verdunkeln. Ueber die moralische Seite zu sprechen, ist unsere Sache. Denn so viel auch die Judenfrage jetzt erörtert wird, was in der Seele der deutschen Juden vorgeht, was vom jüdischen Standpunkt zu den Vorgängen zu sagen ist, kann niemand aussprechen als wir selbst. Die Juden können heute nicht ... sprechen. Alles andere ist ...

... ist eine nationale Frage, und um sie zu lösen, müssen wir sie vor allem zu einer politischen Weltfrage machen, die im Rate der Kulturvölker zu regeln sein wird."

Man müßte Seite um Seite dieser 1897 erschienenen Schrift abschreiben, um zu zeigen: Theodor Herzl war der erste Jude, der unbefangen genug war, den Antisemitismus im Zusammenhang mit der Judenfrage zu betrachten. Und er erkannte, daß nicht durch Vogel-Strauß-Politik, sondern nur durch offene Behandlung der Tatsachen vor aller Welt eine Besserung erzielt werden kann. Gegen nichts hat er so leidenschaftlich Stellung genommen als gegen das, was ihm jetzt unterschoben wird, nämlich gegen den Gedanken, die Juden könnten eine nichtöffentliche Weltverbindung herstellen ...

... gedacht. Wir nehmen sie auf, und wollen daraus ein Ehrenzeichen machen.

Viele Juden hatten am Sonnabend ein schweres Erlebnis. Nicht aus innerem Bekenntnis, nicht aus Stolz auf eine zur eigenen Gemeinschaft, nicht aus Menschheitsleistung, sondern durch den Aufdruck des roten Zettels und des gelben Flecks standen sie plötzlich als Juden da. Von Haus zu Haus gingen die Trupps, beklebten Geschäfte und Schilder, bemalten die Fensterscheiben, 24 Stunden lang waren die deutschen Juden gewissermaßen an den Pranger gestellt. Neben anderen Zeichen und Inschriften sah man auf den ...

V. THE JEWISH BADGE

(117) Three days after the rise of Hitler to power, the German Zionist organ, *Jüdische Rundschau*, proclaimed, "Wear it with pride, this yellow badge," as if its editors had a premonition of the introduction of the yellow badge in passports and other documents, and on Jewish houses, and the Star of David and other distinctive signs to be worn by Jews.

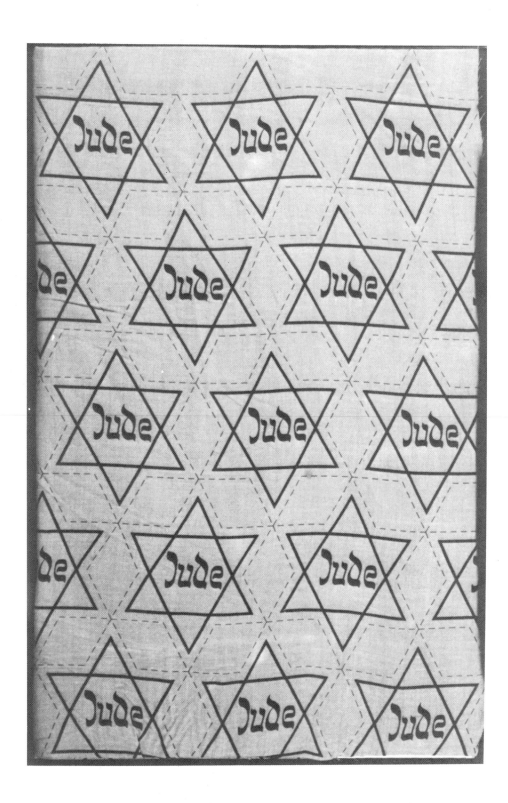

(118) A piece of yellow fabric used for printing the
Star of David, Germany.

DANN DENKE DARAN

was der Jude unserem Volke angetan hat

als er als Urheber und Anführer der Revolte im Jahre 1918 den **Zusammenbruch des deutschen Volkes** verschuldete,

als er dann die maßgeblichen Positionen in der Staatsführung innehatte und durch die Inflation **das Vermögen des deutschen Volkes stahl,**

als er durch seine Herrschaft über die deutsche Wirtschaft brutal und rücksichtslos mehr **als sieben Millionen Deutsche zu Erwerbslosen machte,** um dadurch über billige Arbeitskräfte zu verfügen und so seinen Profit ins Unermeßliche zu steigern,

als er fast die gesamte deutsche Presse in seinen Händen hatte,

als er das Theater, den Film, das gesamte Kulturleben beherrschte und dadurch **das deutsche Volk seelisch vergiften und moralisch verderben wollte.**

Wie einen bösen Traum

haben viele Volksgenossen diese Erinnerungen an die Zeit der größten Not und tiefsten Erniedrigung des deutschen Volkes beiseite geschoben.

Alles das jedoch, was wir als Folge der Judenherrschaft in Deutschland erlebten, ja alles, was wir bisher von den Plänen des Weltjudentums gehört oder erfahren haben, ist nichts gegen die grauenvolle Zukunft, die Juda dem deutschen Volke tatsächlich bereiten will.

Jetzt wurde   im ersten Male offen ausgesprochen, was das Weltju   wünscht:

          uß sterben"

          stehende, fleißige und anständige   und Kinder sollen ausgerottet werden.   ie der amerikanische Jude Theodore   t der Amerikanischen Friedensver   Weltjudentums in seinem Buch „Ger   bt.

(119) First two pages of a four-page pamphlet against Jews with the Jewish badge, Germany.

Der Distriktschef von Krakau

ANORDNUNG

Kennzeichnung der Juden im Distrikt Krakau

Ich ordne an, dass alle Juden im Alter von über 12 Jahren im Distrikt Krakau mit Wirkung vom 1. 12. 1939 ausserhalb ihrer eigenen Wohnung ein sichtbares Kennzeichen zu tragen haben. Dieser Anordnung unterliegen auch nur vorübergehend im Distriktsbereich anwesende Juden für die Dauer ihres Aufenthaltes.

Als Jude im Sinne dieser Anordnung gilt:

1. wer der mosaischen Glaubensgemeinschaft angehört oder angehört hat,
2. jeder, dessen Vater oder Mutter der mosaischen Glaubensgemeinschaft angehört oder angehört hat.

Als Kennzeichen ist am rechten Oberarm der Kleidung und der Überkleidung eine Armbinde zu tragen, die auf weissem Grunde an der Aussenseite einen blauen Zionstern zeigt. Der weisse Grund muss eine Breite von mindestens 10 cm. haben, der Zionstern muss so gross sein, dass dessen gegenüberliegende Spitzen mindestens 8 cm. entfernt sind. Der Balken muss 1 cm. breit sein.

Juden, die dieser Verpflichtung nicht nachkommen, haben strenge Bestrafung zu gewärtigen.

Für die Ausführung dieser Anordnung. Insbesondere die Versorgung der Juden mit Kennzeichen, sind die Ältestenräte verantwortlich.

Krakau, den 18. 11. 1939.

Wächter
Gouverneur

Szef dystryktu krakowskiego

ROZPORZĄDZENIE

Znamionowanie żydów w okręgu Krakowa

Zarządzam z ważnością od dnia 1. XII. 1939, iż wszyscy żydzi w wieku ponad 12 lat winni nosić widoczne znamiona. Rozporządzeniu temu podlegają także na czas ich pobytu przejściowo w obrębie okręgu przebywający żydzi.

Żydem w myśl tego rozporządzenia jest:

1) ten, który jest lub był wyznania mojżeszowego,
2) każdy, którego ojciec, lub matka są lub byli wyznania mojżeszowego.

Znamieniem jest biała przepaska noszona na prawym rękawie ubrania lub odzienia wierzchniego, na której jest niebieska gwiazda sjonistyczna. Przepaska winna mieć szerokość co najmniej 10 cm, gwiazda średnicę 8 cm. Wstążka, z której sporządzono gwiazdę, winna mieć szerokość conajmniej 1 cm.

Niestosujący się do tego zarządzenia zostaną surowo ukarani.

Za wykonanie niniejszego zarządzenia, zwłaszcza za dostarczenie opasek czynię odpowiedzialna Radę starszych.

Kraków, dnia 18. XI. 1939.

(—) *Wächter*
Gubernator

121

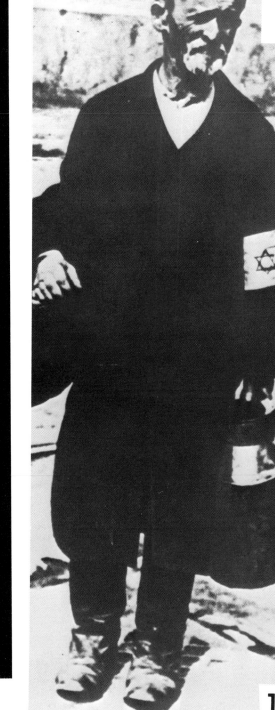

47

122

Wer dieses Zeichen trägt, ist ein Feind unseres Volkes

120

(120) Sticker against Jews wearing the yellow badge, Germany. (121) Order of the German commandant in the district of Cracow that Jews must wear the Jewish badge, November 18, 1939. (122) A Polish Jew with the badge.

Verordnung

Lemberg, 8. Juli 1941.

Die jüdische Bevölkerung über 14 Jahren, welche sich in der Stadt oder im Bezirk Lemberg aufhält, hat ab 15. Juli 1941 als Kennzeichen eine weiße Armbinde mit blauem sechseckigem Stern (Dawidstern) auf dem rechten Oberarm zu tragen.

Jude ist, wer von mindestens drei der Rasse nach volljüdischen Grosseltern abstammt.

Als Jude gilt auch der von zwei volljüdischen Grosselten abstammende jüdische Mischling,

a) der der jüdischen Religionsgemeinschaft angehört oder noch in sie aufgenommen wird,

b) der mit einem Juden verheiratet ist oder sich noch mit einem solchen verheiratet.

Juden, die das Kennzeichen nicht tragen, werden bestraft.

Ausländer fallen nicht unter diese Verordnung.

DER KOMMANDANT
der Stadt Lemberg.

РОЗПОРЯДОК

Львів, 8 липня 1941 р.

Жидівське населення в літах вище 14, що перебуває в місті Львові або у львівській окрузі, має, починаючи від 15. липня 1941 р., носити як відзнаку на правому рамені білу перев'язку з синьою, шестикутньою зіркою (зірка Давида).

Жидом є кожний, хто походить від щонайменше трьох за расою чистожидівських предків.

За жида треба вважати теж жидівського мішанця, що походить від двох чистожидівських предків.

а) того, хто належить до жидівської релігійної громади, або буде принятий до неї,

б) того, хто з жидом одружений або одружиться з жидом.

Жиди, що не носять такої відзнаки, підлягають карі.

До чужоземців цей розпорядок не відноситься.

Командант м. Львова.

Rozporządzenie

Lwów, 8 lipca 1941 r.

Ludność żydowska powyżej lat 14, przebywająca w mieście Lwowie albo w powiecie lwowskim, obowiązana jest nosić, począwszy od 15 lipca 1941, jako odznakę na prawym ramieniu białą opaskę z niebieską sześciokątną gwiazdą (gwiazda Dawida)

Żydem jest każdy, kto pochodzi od conajmniej trzech rasowo czystożydowskich przodków.

Za żyda należy również uważać żydowskiego mieszańca, pochodzącego od dwóch czystożydowskich przodków,

a) tego, kto należy do żydowskiej gminy wyznaniowej albo do niej przyjęty zostanie,

tego, kto pozostaje w związku małżeńskim z żydem albo związek małżeński z żydem zawrze.

Żydzi, nie noszący takiej odznaki, podlegają karze.

Cudzoziemców rozporządzenie to nie dotyczy.

124

KOMENDANT
miasta Lwowa.

Verordnung
vom 14. November 1939

Erhebliche durch die Juden verursachte Mißstände im öffentlichen Leben des Verwaltungsbereichs des Regierungspräsidenten zu Kalisch veranlassen mich, für den Verwaltungsbereich des Regierungspräsidenten zu Kalisch folgendes zu bestimmen:

§ 1

Als besonderes Kennzeichen tragen Juden ohne Rücksicht auf Alter und Geschlecht am rechten Oberarm unmittelbar unter der Achselhöhle eine 10 cm breite Armbinde in Judengelber Farbe.

§ 2

Juden dürfen im Verwaltungsbereich des Regierungspräsidenten zu Kalisch in der Zeit von 17—8 Uhr ihre Wohnung ohne meine besondere Genehmigung nicht verlassen.

§ 3

Zuwiderhandlungen gegen diese Verordnung werden mit dem Tode bestraft. Bei Vorliegen mildernder Umstände kann auf Geldstrafe in unbeschränkter Höhe oder Gefängnis, allein oder in Verbindung miteinander, erkannt werden.

§ 4

Diese Verordnung tritt bis auf die Bestimmung in § 1 sofort, § 1 vom 18. November 1939 ab in Kraft.

Lodz, den 14. November 1939.

123

Der Regierungspräsident zu Kalisch
Uebelhoer

Rozporządzenie
z dnia 14 listopada 1939 r.

Znaczne niedomagania w życiu publicznym obszaru administracyjnego Prezydenta Regencji w Kalisch (w Kaliszu) skłaniają mnie do wydania dla obszaru administracyjnego Prezydenta Regencji w Kalisch (w Kaliszu) następującego rozporządzenia:

§ 1

Jako oznakę szczególną noszą żydzi bez względu na wiek i płeć na prawem ramieniu bezpośrednio pod pachą opaskę szerokości 10 cm koloru żydowsko żółtego.

§ 2

Na obszarze administracyjnym Prezydenta Regencji w Kalisch (w Kaliszu) żydom nie wolno bez mojego szczególnego zezwolenia opuszczać swego mieszkania w czasie od godzin. 17-ej do 8-ej

§ 3

Kto wykracza przeciwko niniejszemu rozporządzeniu, podlega karze śmierci. Jeśli zachodzą okoliczności łagodzące, to może być orzeczona kara pieniężna w nieograniczonej wysokości lub kara więzienia, każda z nich oddzielnie lub obie łącznie.

§ 4

Rozporządzenie niniejsze, prócz postanowienia paragrafu pierwszego, wchodzi natychmiast w życie, a paragraf pierwszy z dniem 18 listopada 1939 r.

Łódź, dnia 14 listopada 1939 r.

Prezydent Regencji w Kalisch (w Kaliszu)
Uebelhoer

(123–125) German orders of Warsaw, Lwów, and Kalisz that Jews must wear the yellow badge.

ANORDNUNG

Betrifft: Kennzeichnung der Juden im Distrikt Warschau.

Ich ordne an, dass alle Juden im Alter von über 12 Jahren im Distrikt Warschau mit Wirkung vom 1.12.1939 ausserhalb ihrer eigenen Wohnung ein sichtbares Kennzeichen zu tragen haben. Dieser Anordnung unterliegen auch nur vorübergehend im Distriktsbereich anwesende Juden für die Dauer ihres Aufenthaltes.

Als Jude im Sinne dieser Anordnung gilt:

1. wer der mosaischen Glaubensgemeinschaft angehört, oder angehört hat,

2. jeder, dessen Vater oder Mutter der mosaischen Glaubensgemeinschaft angehört hat.

Als Kennzeichen ist am rechten Oberarm der Kleidung und der Überkleidung eine Armbinde zu tragen, die auf weissem Grunde an der Aussenseite einen blauen Zionsstern zeigt. Der weisse Grund muss so gross sein, dass dessen gegenüberliegende Spitzen mindestens 8 cm entfernt sind. Der Balken muss 1 cm breit sein.

Juden, die dieser Verpflichtung nicht nachkommen, haben strenge Bestrafung zu gewärtigen.

Für die Ausführung dieser Anordnung, insbesondere die Versorgung der Juden mit Kennzeichen, sind die Ältestenräte verantwortlich.

Die Durchführung obliegt im Bereich der Stadt Warschau dem Stadtpräsidenten, in den Landkreisen den Kreishauptleuten.

Der Chef des Distrikts Warschau
(—) Dr. FISCHER
Gouverneur

ROZPORZĄDZENIE

Dotyczy: oznak dla żydów w obwodzie warszawskim.

Zarządzam, aby wszyscy żydzi zamieszkali w obwodzie warszawskim, nosili widoczne oznaki w czasie przebywania poza własnym mieszkaniem. Zarządzenie to obowiązuje z dn. 1.12.1939 r. i dotyczy wszystkich żydów w wieku ponad lat 12. Temu zarządzeniu podlegają również żydzi przejściowo przebywający w obwodzie warszawskim na czas ich pobytu.

W myśl tego zarządzenia uważa się za żyda tego

1. który należał lub należy do gminy wyznania mojżeszowego.

2. którego ojciec lub matka należą lub należeli do gminy wyznania mojżeszowego.

Jako oznakę należy nosić na prawym ramieniu ubrania i przedstawiającą niebieską gwiazdę syjońska na białym tle. musi być tak duże, aby przeciwległe końce gwiazdy od siebie przynajmniej o 8 cm. Szerokość ramienia gwiazdy ma wynosić 1 cm.

Żydzi, którzy tego zarządzenia nie spełnią będą surowo karani.

Za wykonanie tego zarządzenia, zwłaszcza za zaopatrzenie żydów w oznaki, odpowiedzialna jest Rada Starszych gminy żydowskiej.

Wykonanie na terenie miasta Warszawy należy do Prezydenta miasta, a w powiatach wiejskich do naczelników powiatów.

Szef obwodu warszawskiego
(—) Dr. FISCHER
Gubernator

125

Bekanntmachung

Auf Anordnung des Generalgouverneurs über die Kennzeichnung der Juden wird folgendes bekannt gegeben:

Von heute ab haben alle Juden — ohne Ausnahme — die vorgeschriebene weise Binde mit dem Zionsstern zu tragen.

Die von mir gewährten Ausnahmebescheinigungen sind ab sofort ungültig.

Tarnow, den 18. Dezember 1939.

Der Stadtkommissar der kreisfreien Stadt Tarnow
In Vertretung

ENGEL
komm. Stadtdirektor.

OGŁOSZENIE

Powołując się na zarządzenie Generalnego Gubernatora dotyczące znamionowania Żydów, podaję do wiadomości co następuje:

Z dniem dzisiejszym wszyscy Żydzi bez wyjątku winni nosić białą przepaskę z gwiazdą syjonistyczną.

Udzielone przezemnie zwolnienia od noszenia przepaski są od dnia dzisiejszego nieważne.

Tarnów, dnia 18 grudnia 1939.

Der Stadtkommissar der kreisfreien Stadt Tarnow
In Vertretung

ENGEL

127

Feldkommandantur 581.
Lomza, den 4. Juli 1941.

ANORDNUNG.

Sämtliche Juden und Jüdinnen vom 12. Lebensjahr an haben auf Brust und Rücken einen runden gelben Fleck von mindestens 10 cm Durchmesser sichtbar zu tragen. Diese Massnahme muss bis zum 7 Juli 1941 durchgeführt sein.

Zuwiderhandelnde werden bestraft.

Krüger
Major u. Feldkommandant.

Komenda Polowa 581.
Lomża, 4. lipca 1941.

ZARZĄDZENIE.

Wszyscy Żydzi i Żydówki od 12 roku życia począwszy, obowiązani są nosić naszyte na piersiach i plecach żółte, okrągłe łaty o średnicy conajmniej 10 cm. Łaty te mają być zawsze widoczne. Zarządzenie to ma być wykonane do dnia 7 lipca 1941.

Nie stosujący się do niniejszego zarządzenia będą ukarani.

Krüger
Major i Komendant Polowy.

126

ANORDNUNG Nr. 1

1) Sämtliche Juden beiderlei Geschlechts der Stadt Wilna sind verpflichtet, zu ihrer Kennzeichnung je einen gelben Zionsstern auf der linken Brustseite und auf dem Rücken zu tragen.

2) Der jüdischen Bevölkerung wird das Betreten der Gehsteige untersagt. Die Juden haben den rechtsseitigen Rand der Fahrstrasse einzuhalten und hintereinander zu gehen.

3) Der jüdischen Bevölkerung wird der Aufenthalt auf Promenadenwegen und in allen öffentlichen Grünanlangen verboten. Desgleichen wird der jüdischen Bevölkerung die Benutzung der aufgestellten Ruhebänke untersagt.

4) Der jüdischen Bevölkerung wird die Benutzung aller öffentlichen Verkehrsmittel wie Autotaxen, Pferdedroschken und Autobussen, Personendampfern und ähnlicher Fahrzeuge untersagt. Die Eigentümer bezw. Halter der öffentlichen Fahrzeuge sind verpflichtet, an sichtbarer Stelle der Fahrzeuge ein Plakat zu befestigen mit der Aufschrift: „Für Juden verboten".

5) Zuwiderhandelnde gegen diese Verordnung werden schärfstens bestraft.

6) Diese Anordnung tritt mit dem heutigen Tage in Kraft.

Der Gebietskommissar der Stadt Wilna
gez. Hingst.

Wilna, den 2. August 1941.

PRIVALOMAS NUTARIMAS Nr. 1

1) Vilniaus miesto abiejų lyčių žydai, kad atskirti, yra įpareigojami ant kairės krutinės pusės ir nugaros nešioti geltoną Siono žvaigždę.

2) Žydų tautybės gyventojams draudžiama naudotis šaligatviais. Žydai privalo gatvėse eiti važiuojamojo kelio dešiniuoju kraštu vienas po kito.

3) Žydų tautybės gyventojams draudžiama naudotis visomis pasivaikščiojimo bei poilsio vietomis ir viešaisiais parkais bei skverais. Taip pat jiems draudžiama naudotis viešose vietose išstatytais suolais.

4) Žydų tautybės gyventojams draudžiama naudotis visomis viešosiomis susisiekimo priemonėmis, kaip auto taksi, vežikais, autobusais, garlaiviais ir pan. Visi viešojo naudojimo susisiekimo priemonių savininkai arba nuomotojai privalo nurodytų priemonių matomoje vietoje iškabinti skelbimą su užrašu: „Žydams draudžiama".

5) Nesilaikantieji šio nutarimo nuostatų bei jiems priešstaraujantieji bus griežtai baudžiami.

6) Šis nutarimas galioja nuo šios dienos.

Vilniaus miesto Apygardos Komisaras
HINGST

ZARZĄDZENIE OBOWIĄZUJĄCE Nr. 1

1) W m. Wilnie żydzi dla odróżnienia od reszty ludności zobowiązani nosić po lewej stronie piersi i na plecach gwiazdę siońską.

2) Żydom zabrania się przy chodzeniu po mieście używać chodników, lecz tylko jezdni. Chodzić żydzi muszą tylko prawą stroną i tylko gęsiego (jeden za drugim).

3) Mieszkańcom miasta narodowości żydowskiej zabrania się korzystać z miejskich parków, skwerów lub innych miejsc wypoczynkowych. Takie wzbrania się korzystać z ławek znajdujących się w miejscach publicznych.

4) Mieszkańcom narodowości żydowskiej zabrania się korzystać ze wszelkich środków lokomocji jak to: z dorożek, taksówek, autobusów, parostatków itp. Właściciele wszelkich środków lokomocji użyteczności publicznej winni w widocznym miejscu powyżej oznaczonych środków lokomocji umieścić wywieszkę następującej treści: „żydom wzbroniono".

5) Niewykonanie niniejszego zarządzenia będzie surowo karane.

6) Zarządzenie niniejsze wchodzi w życie z dniem dzisiejszym.

Komisarz Okręgu Wileńskiego
HINGST

128

(126–128) German orders of Lomza, Tarnów, and Vilna that Jews must wear the Jewish badge.

131

129

(129) A Jewess with the yellow badge in Przemysl, Poland. (130) A Jewess selling badges in Warsaw. (131) Jews wearing yellow triangles in parts of Poland.

130

133

132

134

Jews wearing the badge in the Bedzin ghetto (132),
in Odessa on the way to deportation **(133)**, and in
Yugoslavia **(134)**.

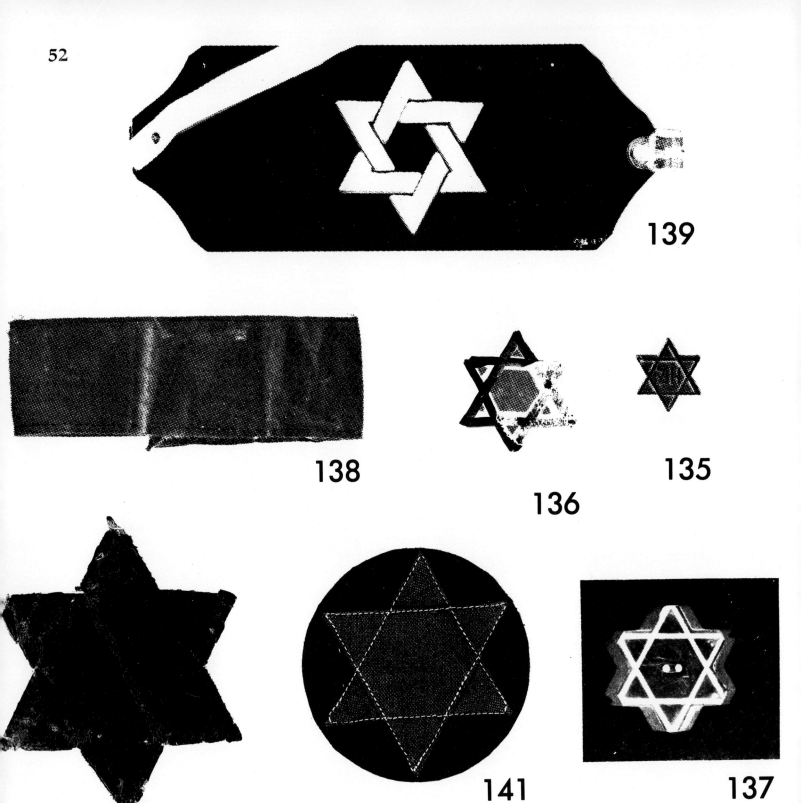

139

138

136

135

140

141

137

(135–136) The yellow badge in Slovakia: blue Star of David on a yellow background and a yellow star. (137) In Bulgaria: black on a yellow background and in the form of a yellow button. (138) In parts of Greece and other countries: yellow armband. (139) The badge in East and Upper Silesia: blue Star of David on a white armband. (140) The yellow Star of David in Bulgaria, Hungary, parts of Poland, Greece, Lithuania. (141) The badge in Rumania: yellow star on a black background.

146

143

144

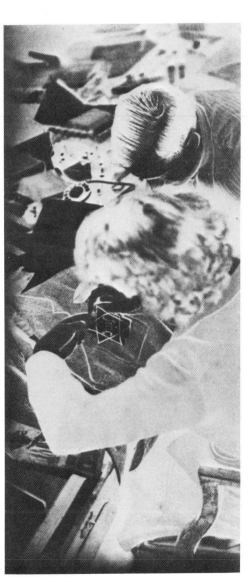

A QUAND L'ETOILE JAUNE
POUR LES JUIFS?

142

Quand se décidera-t-on
à marquer les Juifs ?

The Jewish badge in France: **(142)** "For when the yellow star for Jews?" "When will one decide to mark the Jews?" Slogans in the French magazine *L'Appel*, February–April 1942. **(143)** The badge in France: a black Star of David with the inscription *Juif* [Jew] on a yellow background. **(144)** Distribution of the yellow badge in a Paris police station. **(145)** Sewing on the yellow badge. **(146)** Caricature in the French magazine *Au Pilori* of June 4, 1942 ("What a shame, Abraham, we are marked!" "The shame is not important, but what is insane is that they are not even fabricated by us").

145

147

148

149

150

(147) A Jewish mother and her daughter with yellow badges on a Paris street. (148) Anna Schwartzbard (widow of Sholem Schwartzbard, who assassinated Simon Petlura, the leader of the pogromist Ukrainian army) with the badge. (149) A group of French soldiers in the German P.O.W. camp Stalag IV B at Mahlberg. In the center of the first row: the dentist Lt. N. Chatt with the yellow star. (150) Franco-Jewish soldier in a German P.O.W. camp with the yellow star.

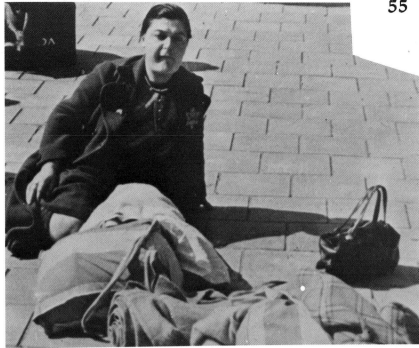

154

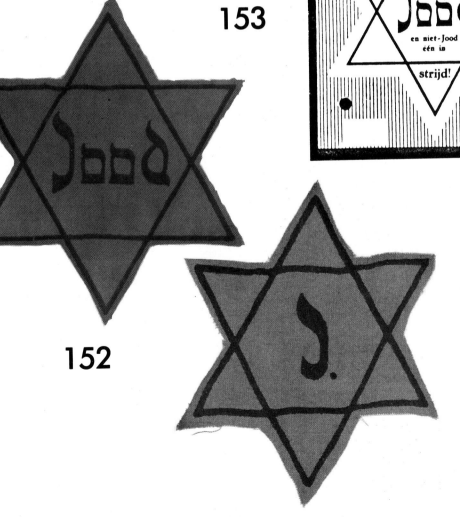

153

155

152

151

The Jewish badge in Belgium and Holland: (151) Belgium: a black Star of David with a *J* in the center on a yellow background. (152) Holland: a black Star of David with *Jood* [Jew] in the center on a yellow background. (153–154) Dutch Jewish women wearing the badge on the way for deportation. (155) A Dutch Jewish badge with the inscription "Jew and non-Jew stand united in their struggle," distributed by the Dutch underground, 1942.

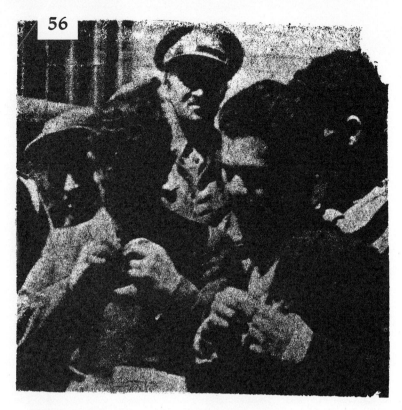

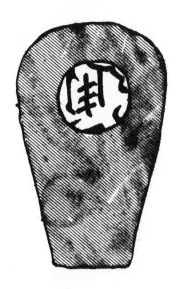

159

158

156

157

(156) The Jewish badge of forced laborers in the ghetto of Skole (Poland) and other places. (157) A small Star of David made of metal and attached to a black piece of leather, made by the internees of the Waldenburg camp, Lower Silesia, awaiting their liberators. (158) Jewish boys at a forced-labor camp in Kairouan (Tunisia) ripping off the yellow badge after the liberation. (159) The Jewish badge in the ghetto of Shanghai.

Liste der jüdischen Vornamen

Regelung auch für jüdische Träger von deutschen Vornamen

Im Reichsgesetzblatt ist die Zweite Verordnung zur Durchführung des Gesetzes über die Aenderung von Familiennamen und Vornamen erschienen, die die Führung von Vornamen durch Juden regelt. Sie bestimmt, dass den Juden, die deutsche Staatsangehörige oder staatenlos sind, in Zukunft nur solche Vornamen beigelegt werden dürfen, die den vom Reichsminister des Innern herausgegebenen Richtlinien entsprechen.

Diese Richtlinien sind in dem Runderlass vom 23. August 1938 bekanntgegeben, der im Reichsministerialblatt für die innere Verwaltung veröffentlicht ist. Wie die unten abgedruckte Zusammenstellung ergibt, sind darin nur solche Vornamen enthalten, die im deutschen Volk als typisch jüdisch angesehen werden. Juden, die eine fremde Staatsangehörigkeit besitzen, werden von der Vorschrift nicht betroffen.

Soweit Juden zur Zeit Vornamen führen, die nicht in den Richtlinien verzeichnet sind, müssen sie vom 1. Januar 1939 ab zusätzlich einen weiteren Vornamen annehmen, und zwar männliche Personen den Vornamen Israel, weibliche Personen den Vornamen Sara. Sie müssen hiervon bis zum 31. Januar 1939 den Standesamten, die ihre Geburt und ihre Heirat beurkundet haben, sowie der für ihren Wohnsitz oder gewöhnlichen Aufenthalt zuständigen Ortspolizeibehörde schriftlich Anzeige erstatten. Bei geschäftsunfähigen oder in der Geschäftsfähigkeit beschränkten Personen trifft die Verpflichtung zur Anzeige den gesetzlichen Vertreter. Sofern es im Rechts- und Geschäftsverkehr üblich ist, den Namen anzugeben, müssen Juden stets auch wenigstens einen ihrer Vornamen anführen. Sind sie zur Annahme des zusätzlichen Vornamens Israel oder Sara verpflichtet, so haben sie auch diesen Vornamen zu führen. Bei Zuwiderhandlungen gegen diese Vorschriften sind Gefängnis- oder Geldstrafen angedroht.

Männliche Vornamen

Als jüdische Vornamen sind in dem Runderlass des Reichsministers des Innern bekanntgegeben: a) **Männliche Vornamen:** Abel, Abieser, Abimelech, Abner, Absalom, Ahab, Ahasja, Ahasver, Akiba, Amon, Anschel, Aron, Asabel, Asaria, Ascher, Asriel, Assur, Athaija, Awigdor, Awrum; **Bachja,** Barak, Baruch, Benaja, Berek, Berl, Boas, Bud; **Chaggai,** Chai, Chajin, Chamor, Chananja, Chanoch, Chaskel, Chawa, Chiel; **Dan,** Denny; **Efim,** Efraim, Ehud, Eisig, Eli, Elias, Elihu, Eliser, Eljakim, Elkan, Enoch, Esau, Esra, Ezechiel; **Faleg,** Feibisch, Feirel, Feitel, Feiwel, Feleg; **Gad,** Gdaleo, Gedalja, Gerson, Gideon; **Habakuk,** Hagai, Hemor, Henoch, Herodes, Hesekiel, Hillel, Hiob, Hosea; **Isaac,** Isai, Isachar, Isboseth, Isidor, Ismael, Israel, Itzig; **Jachiel,** Jaffe, Jakar, Jakusiel, Jescheskel, Jechiel, Jehu, Jehuda, Jehusiel, Jeremia, Jerobeam, Jesaja, Jethro, Jiftach, Jizchak, Joab, Jochanan, Joel, Jomteb, Jona, Jonathan, Josia, Juda; **Kainan,** Kaiphas, Kaleb, Korach; **Laban,** Lazarus, Leew, Leiser, Levi, Lewek, Lot, Lupu; **Machol,** Maim, Malchisua, Maleachi, Manasse, Mardochai, Mechel, Menachem, Moab, Mochain, Mordeschaj, Mosche, Moses; **Nachschon,** Nachum, Naftali, Nathan, Naum, Nazury, Nehab, Nehemia, Nissim, Noa, Nochem; **Obadja,** Orew, Oscher, Osias; **Peisach,** Pinchas, Pinkus; **Rachmiel,** Ruben; **Sabbatai,** Sacher, Sallum, Sally, Salo, Salomon, Salusch, Samaja, Sami, Samuel, Sandel, Saudik, Saul, Schalom, Schaul, Schinul, Schmul, Schneur, Schoachana, Scholem, Sebulon, Semi, Sered, Sichem, Sirach, Simson; **Teit,** Tewele; **Uri,** Uria, Uriel; **Zadek,** Zedekia, Zephanja, Zeruja, Zewi.

Weibliche Vornamen

Abigail; **Baschewa,** Beile, Bela, Bescha, Bihri, Bilba, Breine, Briewe, Brocha; **Chana,** Chawa, Cheiche, Cheile, Chinke; **Deiche,** Dewaara, Driesel, **Egele;** Faugel, Feigle, Feile, Fradchen, Fradel, Frommet; **Geilchen,** Gelea, Ginendel, Gittel, Gole; **Hadasse,** Hale, Hannacha, Hitzel; **Jachel,** Jachewad, Jedidja, Jente, Jezabel, Judis, Jyske, Jyttel; **Keile,** Kreindel; **Lane,** Leie, Libsche, Libe, Liwie; **Machle,** Mathel, Milkele, Mindel; **Nacha,** Nachme; **Peirche,** Pesschen, Pesse, Pessel, Pirle; **Rachel,** Rause, Rebekka, Rechel, Reha, Reichel, Reisel, Reitzge, Reitzsche, Riwki; **Sara,** Scharne, Scheindel, Scheine, Schewa, Schlämche, Semche, Simche, Slowe, Sprinze; **Tana,** Telze, Tirze, Treibel; **Zerel,** Zilla, Zimle, Zine, Zipora, Zirel, Zorthel.

Abgesehen von diesen Sondervorschriften über die Vornamen der Juden, sollen nach dem sonstigen Inhalt des Runderlasses Kinder deutscher Staatsangehöriger in Zukunft grundsätzlich nur deutsche Vornamen erhalten. Namen, ursprünglich ausländischer Herkunft, die seit Jahrhunderten in Deutschland als Vornamen verwendet werden und völlig eingedeutscht sind — wie Hans Joachim, Peter, Julius, Elisabeth, Maria, Sofie, Charlotte — gelten als deutsche Vornamen. Nichtdeutsche Vornamen sollen nur dann zugelassen werden, wenn ein besonderer Grund dies rechtfertigt: so z. B. Zugehörigkeit zu einem nichtdeutschen Volkstum, Familienüberlieferung, verwandtschaftliche Beziehungen.

Deutsches Reich

J

Kennkarte
162

(160) Ordinance restricting the use of first names of German Jews. (161) Certificate that a Vienna Jew added *Israel* to his first name. By order of the Third Reich, all Jews had to do so. (162) German foreign passports were marked with *J*. This was done at the request of Swiss authorities desiring to facilitate the refusal of entry of German-Jewish refugees.

161

GENERALGOUVERNEMENT
GENERALNE GUBERNATORSTWO

KENNKARTE

KARTA ROZPOZNAWCZA

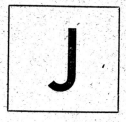

J

163

PERSONAL-AUSWEIS
DOWÓD OSOBISTY Nr. 69

164

165

166

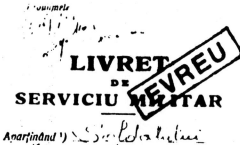

Passports and other identification papers belonging to Jews were marked with *J* and other distinctive marks: **(163–164)** Poland. **(165)** Rumania. **(166)** Belgium.

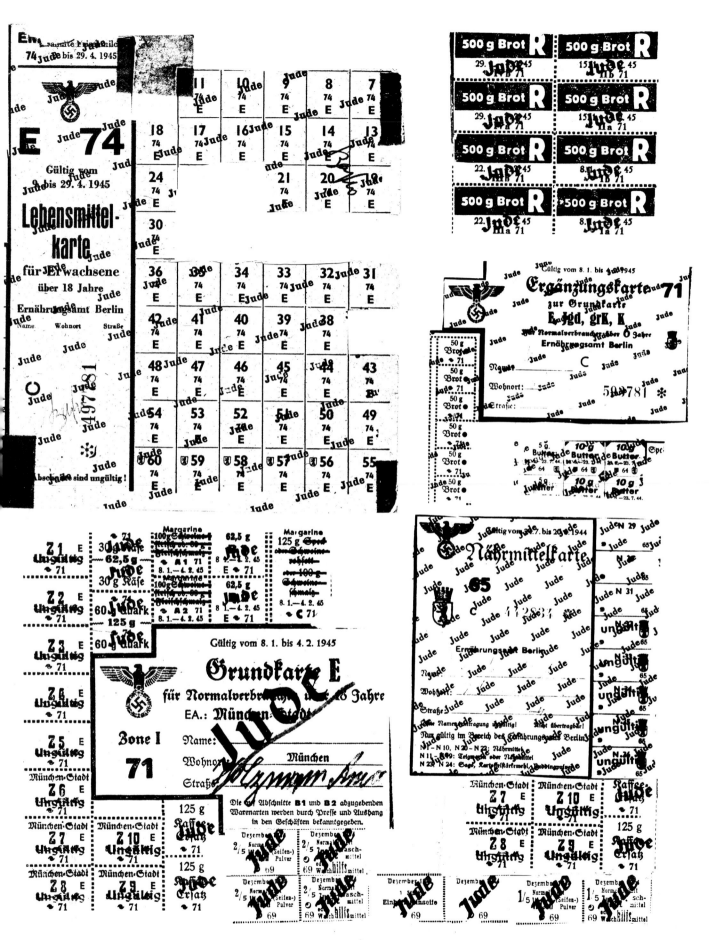

(167) Ration cards for German Jews marked *Jude*.

168

16

Die Reichspropagandaleitung der NSDAP

lädt zu der am Donnerstag, dem 28. November 1940, im

UFA=PALAST AM ZOO

ftattfindenden Feftaufführung des dokumentarifchen Films

Der ewige Jude

ein.

Der Film läuft 16 Uhr und 18.30 Uhr in verfchiedenen Faffungen.

Da in der Vorftellung um 18.30 Uhr zufäglich Originalaufnahmen von jüdifchen Tier=
fchächtungen gezeigt werden, wird empfindfamen Gemütern die gekürzte Faffung in
der Vorftellung um 16 Uhr empfohlen.
Frauen ift der Zutritt ebenfalls nur zu der Vorftellung um 16 Uhr geftattet.

Zwecks Zutellung der Eintrittskarten wird gebeten, beiliegende Beftellkarte bis zum
23. Nov. einzufenden. Verfpätet eingehende Zufagen können nicht berüdfichtigt werden.

Nichts für empfindsame Gemüter.

170

VI. THE ANTISEMITE AMUSES HIMSELF
(Propaganda through films, theatre, sports, etc.)

(168) Cartoon on the Jews' control of the theatre, 1935. (169) Illustration for an article by Dr. W. Grau on Jewish art. (170) Invitation to a Berlin showing of the film *The Eternal Jew*, November 28, 1940. "Not for sensitive souls."

De film „De eeuwige Jood", welke binnenkort uit-
komt, toont het wezen en de geschiedkundige ont-
wikkeling van het Jodendom met een duidelijke
karakteriseering van de Joodsche raskenmerken. De
waarde ervan ligt hierin, dat zij de altijd gelijk-
blijvende Joodsche doelstellingen belicht en de
Joodsche camouflage-pogingen, al zijn deze ook nog
zoo goed gelukt, ontmaskert. Zij wekt in den bioscoop-
bezoeker een instinctmatigen afkeer van dat vreemde

173

171

The Eternal Jew: (171) The *Berliner Beobachter*
announces the success of the film, December 9, 1938.
(172–173) Dutch posters.

172

175

176

(174–175) Posters for the antisemitic film *Jud Süss*.
(176) The *Berliner Illustrirte Zeitung* included photos of recent deportations of Jews besides scenes from the film.

174

179

178

180

177

(177) "Jews do not belong in the German film," *Fränkische Tageszeitung*, June 25, 1938. **(178)** Special issue of the *Weltkampf* against Jews in the film. **(179)** Shakespeare's drama *The Merchant of Venice* was used for anti-Jewish propaganda. Shown here is the actor Werner Kraus in the role of Shylock. *Berliner Illustrirte Zeitung*, June 3, 1943. **(180)** Cover of Dr. E. Frenzel's pamphlet *Jews in the Theater*.

184

182

Das gefällt den Amerikanern und der Filmjude macht damit sein Geschäft.

181

185

(181) A Nazi theatrical troupe impersonating Jewish physicians with bottles labeled "poison," judges and lawyers taking bribes, and parents selling girl children into prostitution, parading through the streets of Cologne on a "Rose Monday" observance. Map on side of the wagon shows Jews fleeing Cologne for Palestine. (182) Pictures prepared by the German propaganda machine: Jews using sex for American vaudeville business; a man's sex was added to this picture of an actress *(left)*. (183) leaflet protesting against showing Friedrich Wolf's *Prof. Mannheim* at the Zurich Municipal Theater, 1934. (184) Cover of a French book against Jews in the movies and theatre, 1941. (185) Antisemitic play in the Budapest National Theatre, 1944.

183

Ein neuer, unerhörter Skandal

"Prof. Mannheim", das semitische Hetzstück, als "Volksvorstellung" im Zürcher Stadttheater

1.15 p.m. BATAVIA. Commentary in English. **188**
(EXTRACTS)

THE TYRRANY OF THE JEWS: The people of America, Australia
and Britain have been told to fear the totalitarian dictator-
ships of Germany, Italy and Nippon. Russia may be left out
of the present discussion, because the Government of Russia
is a dictatorship imposed by Communism. In addition, the
Russians are fighting their own war against the Germans, and
can, therefore, not be regarded as true Allies of Britain and
the U.S. .... Three years of war have shown that behind
the blissful picture of democratic freedom lies national
inefficiency, and national discord. Behind the grim picture
of Fascist brutality, as painted by democratic leaders, there
lies efficiency, aliveness, progressiveness and freedom.
After the 1914-18 war, Britain and America believed that
Germany had been utterly crushed, and the Versailles treaty
saw to that. But in the years which have passed since,
Germany has made great economic strides, far outstepping
British pedestrian pace. Germany has also built up a
powerful economic and military machine .... Nippon
has already had seven years of war in freeing China from
Communism and driving from China the domination and
exploitation of British and American imperialism. Yet,
since the outbreak of the Pacific war, Nippon has conquered
more territory. This, surely, is proof of the efficiency
of totalitarian governments, where the people sacrifice all
selfish interest to national efficiency ...... Wherever there
is a war, the Jews make money. The name of Bernard Baruch
has now cropped up again, following his recent appointment as
head of the U.S. Rubber Investigation Committee. This is the
same Bernard Baruch, who was so bitterly criticised at the
end of the last war. Now he is at his old games again,
juggling munitions, profiting on war materials .... The Jew,
in centuries long past, was driven from his national home by
the wise men of the East. Although the Jews have lived in
every country since, they have owed allegiance to none.
British Jews have no loyalty to Britain. Australian Jews have
no loyalty to Australia. American Jews have no loyalty to
America. They are Jews, and Jews only ...... Herr Hitler
showed true genius when he made one of the primary aims of
his regime the explusion of all parasite Jews from Germany.
The progress which Germany has since made supports the
justice of this Nazi campaign ..... The Jews are known in
Britain, in Australia and America for their shady business
methods and dubious transactions. Many of the numerous
dishonest company promoters are Jews. Money-lending, as
usury, is almost entirely in the hands of the Jews. The
Jews never produce anything, they merely live as parasites on
the labour of others ..... In Palestine the Jews have gone
far beyond the limits of the Balfour Mandate ..... You may be
sure that the wealthy Jews, who are pretending to support the
war effort, are demanding a tremendous price .... If Britain,
Australia, and America should win this war on paper, they
still will lose the war to the wealthy Jews of Britain,

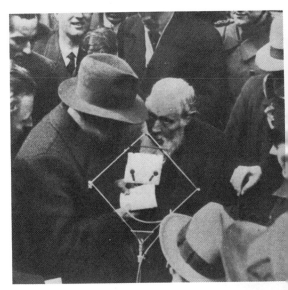

186

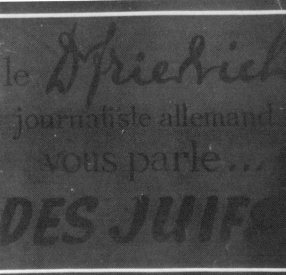

187

Antisemitic propaganda on radio. **(186)** An old Jew
of Berlin is forced to declare that Jews were not
maltreated. **(187)** Cover of book containing the
antisemitic speeches of the German journalist Friedrich on the French radio, 1942. **(188)** Antisemitic
speech on the Tokyo radio, Sept. 16, 1942. The
transcript was made by the Australian monitoring
post in Batavia, Dutch East Indies (now Jakarta,
Indonesia).

ÉDITIONS

LE PONT

NSDAP Nachrichten-Dienst.

Ortsgruppe Duisburg-Neudorf-Nord

Herausgeber: Hermann Hey...

Erscheint wöchentlich. Preis 5 Pfg. August 1933. 24.Folge. 1.Jahrgang.

Der tote Jude.

Deutsche und jüdische Turnvereine/Fritz Rosenfelder ist vernünftig und hängt sich auf.

In Cannstatt in Württemberg wurde vor kurzem der Jude Fritz Rosenfelder aus dem dortigen deutschen Turnverein ausgeschlossen. Das ist eine Sache, so selbstverständlich, dass man darüber eigentlich gar kein Wort verlieren sollte.

Dies hat der Jude Fritz Rosenfelder aus Cannstatt nicht verstehen können. Er hat bisher als Jude den deutschen Turnverein in Cannstatt geleitet und es kam scheinbar in seinem Judenhirn der Gedanke gar nicht auf, dass dies eine grosse Anmassung und Unverschämtheit ist. Als er nun unumgänglicherweise von den Cannstattern nach vollzogener Revolution ausgeschlossen wurde, war er so tief beleidigt, dass er sich in Abrahams Schoss zurückzog. Wie er starb, wissen wir nicht, er wird sich wohl aufgehängt haben. In seiner jüdisch-"auserwählten" Naivität hinterliess er, um Eindruck zu schinden, auch einen Abschiedsbrief. Er lautet:

Ihr lieben Freunde!
Hierdurch mein letztes Lebewohl!

Ein deutscher Jude konnte es nicht über sich bringen zu leben in dem Bewusstsein, von der Bewegung, von der das nationale Deutschland die Rettung erhofft, als Vaterlandsverräter betrachtet zu werden! Ich gehe ohne Hass und Groll! Ein inniger Wunsch beseelt mich: Möge in Bälde die Vernunft Einkehr halten! Da mir bis dahin überhaupt keine - meinem Empfinden entsprechende - Tätigkeit möglich ist, versuche ich durch meinen Freitod meine christlichen Freunde aufzurütteln. Wie es in uns deutschen Juden aussieht, mögt Ihr aus meinem Schritt ersehen. Wie viel lieber hätte ich mein Leben für mein Vaterland gegeben! Trauert nicht, sondern versucht aufzuklären und der Wahrheit zum Siege zu verhelfen. So erweist Ihr mir die grösste Ehre.

Wenn der Jude Fritz Rosenfelder geglaubt hat, damit die Deutschen in ihrer Einstellung zur jüdischen Rasse andern Sinnes werden zu lassen, dann ist er umsonst gestorben. Aber wir denken jetzt, nachdem er tot ist, unsererseits ebenfalls an ihm "ohne Hass und Groll". Im Gegenteil, wir freuen uns über ihn und wir haben nichts dagegen, wenn seine Rassegenossen sich in der gleichen Weise empfehlen. Dann hat nämlich tatsächlich "die Vernunft in Deutschland Einkehr gehalten" und die Judenfrage ist auf einfache und friedliche Weise gelöst. Wir sind dann auch bereit, den Dahingeschiedenen das letzt Geleite zu geben und zu Ehren Jahwes drei donnernde Salven in die Luft zu schiessen.

190

Ich erkläre hiermit auf Ehre und Gewissen, daß ich deutsch-a... Abstammung und frei von jüdischem oder farbigem Rasseeinschl... und erkläre mich hiermit bereit, den Pflichten, die mir bei der ...reitung und nach dem Erwerb des Abzeichens auf Grund der ...führungsbestimmungen erwachsen, gewissenhaft nachzukommen.

...heim den 27. 9. 1937

Eigenhändige Unterschrift

Der Inhaber dieses Leistungsbuches ist nach den "Richtlinien... die ärztliche Untersuchung der Bewerber um das SA-Sport-Abzei... vorschriftsmäßig untersucht worden. Seine Geländesport-Tauglich... ist mit Note 1 bewertet worden und wird hiermit von mir ...raining für den Erwerb des SA-Sport-Abzeichens gemäß den ...führungsbestimmungen zugelassen.

den 27. 9. 1937

SA-Sportabz.
Prüfer
7292...

Der ärztliche Berater

Leistungsprüfung.

Gruppe I: Leibesübungen.

Übung 1. 100 m-Lauf	15	Sek.	2	10 Sek.	6	Punkte
Übung 2. Weitsprung	4	m	—	cm	6	Punkte
Übung 3. Kugelstoßen	10	m	70	cm	6	Punkte
Übung 4. Keulen-Weitwurf	35	m			8	Punkte
Übung 5. 3000 m-Lauf	14	Min.	20	Sek.	1	Punkt

Der Bewerber erhält die Note nicht mit insgesamt 27 Punkte

Unterschrift 62559 Lehrschein-Nr. 7.11.37 Prüfungstag

Gruppe I 27 Punkte × 3 für Gesamtwertung = 81 Pun...

19

Der internationale Boxsport

sieht, bei Licht besehen, so aus, wie ihn unser Bild zeigt

189

Antisemitism in sports. **(189)** Jews exploit boxing sport. Cartoon in *Juda*, May 1935. **(190)** The Nazi *Nachrichten Dienst* [Information Service] published by the local group of Duisburg-Neudorf North of August 1934 announced the suicide of the Jew Fritz Rosenfelder because he was expelled from the local sports society. **(191)** The record of accomplishments of a member of a sports club contains a statement that he is of Aryan descent, 1937.

LE JUIF ET LA PRATIQUE DU SPORT

Le Juif et le Sport ? On ne pouvait pourtant pas retenir ce titre, car on trouvait des éléments aussi inconciliables, aussi résolument étrangers l'un à l'autre.

Le sport, c'est, par excellence, l'activité désintéressée.

Le Juif est la cupidité incarnée.

Le sport, c'est l'effort généreux, et sa perpétuelle recherche d'une occasion de se surpasser.

Le Juif répugne à toute espèce de fatigue physique, surtout dans le seul but de renouveler une énergie qu'il pourrait dépenser à guetter l'occasion d'un profit, et sa vie se passe à guetter l'occasion du Juif.

En sport, on s'affronte sans arrière-pensée. Le calcul préside à tous les actes du Juif.

Le sport implique la soumission absolue à la règle du jeu.

Le Juif cherche sans cesse le biais pour tourner la loi.

Le sport, c'est l'école de l'abnégation, le sacrifice de l'individu au rendement de l'équipe.

Le Juif est fait une loi de ne tirer le plus possible de la collectivité.

On pourrait poursuivre, mais ces principes, dont l'évidence n'est pas contestable, nous en dispensent, et il faut admettre que le titre « Les Juifs et le Sport » juxtapose deux termes qui sont faits pour aller ensemble comme l'eau et le feu.

Ce qui ne veut pas dire qu'il n'y a pas eu de Juifs dans le sport.

Dans bien d'autres voies pour lesquelles ils n'étaient pas faits, on les trouvait, grouillants, et, comment ! Et il fallait voir les résultats ! Des professions qui, à l'origine, étaient des sacerdoces, comme la médecine ou le barreau, devenaient avec eux des entreprises de fraude ou d'escroquerie. Le théâtre, cet art sacré, se changeait, sous leur coupe, en quelque chose d'innommable qui tenait de la gargote, parce qu'on y servait les plus nauséabonds brouets, et de l'hôtel borgne, où l'on reçoit n'importe qui sans même renouveler le linge. Tous les arts, d'ailleurs, que leur ankylosie les met pourvus dans ce qu'ils ont, jeunes, ils prospèrent, sans ce patronage, que leurs soins, dénaturés, vidés de sens et avilis, afin que le Juif pût les exploiter par le déploiement de son unique talent : trafiquer et y briller par son don accessoire : faire l'article. (Tout mercanti fieffé se double d'un péroreur.)

En leurs mains, cinéma, peinture, littérature, architecture, danse, radio, etc., se trouvaient si bizarrement orientés que les Juifs arrivaient à y donner l'illusion qu'ils désintaient une manière d'originalité. Celle parbleu ! — du sauvage, qui, faisant litière des conditions essentielles de la création, mie tout ce qui l'a précédé parce que c'est cela même qui la condamne et donne la mesure vraie des menus ordures qu'il dénomme ses œuvres.

LE SPORT C'EST DU RÉEL

Mais avec le sport, pas une science exacte. A ce passe.

Le sport, lui, est une science exacte. A ce titre, il défiait les artifices du Juif. Je parle du sport actif, de celui qui se passe sur le terrain. Là, il ne suffit pas d'argumenter et de bonimenter. Là tabarinades sont sans effet. On peut, à la rigueur, persuader, par force de vociférations, qu'un bloc dégrossi par Epstein comporte plus d'intentions et de génie que la Moïse de Michel-Ange; on peut, pourvu qu'il y ait dans toute une ligne caqueter que Bloch dans le jeu et parader, avec sa nullité en sautoir ou l'Iliade; on peut partout violer la règle en prétendant qu'elle est le Verbe même; on peut, si l'on dispose des cliques et des tam-

tam, bourrer, à la longue ces mensonges dans la tête de tous les auditeurs de radio et lecteurs de gazette; on peut tout cela, et on peut tout falsifier; mais on ne peut faire que, dans une course en ligne, le second arrive le premier.

Dans le monde truqué, où Israël nous avait, avant la guerre, imposé ses balances à faux poids qui l'autorisaient à poser au surhomme, le sport faisait exception. Là, pas de magie, pas d'incantations qui tiennent. Nul raisonnement tarabiscoté de docteur talmudique que s'emberlificote les pieds dans sa barbe ne pouvait faire que le perdant fût le vainqueur et que le dernier n'eût pas tout le lot devant lui.

Les considérations philosophiques, psychologiques, psychiatriques, psychanalyti-

et deux persistaient à faire quatre et où ce total excédait obstinément trois !

Il n'est pas sûr que cela aurait duré. Le sport aurait peut-être fini par être rectifié, embrouillé comme le reste. Mais toujours est-il que nous n'en étions pas encore là, que le Juif n'avait pu changer encore l'esprit du vrai sport, celui qui comptait, celui d'après lequel on pouvait prendre sa mesure.

Pour s'y attaquer, il manquait peut-être d'expérience.

Dame ! celle-ci ne s'acquière pas en regardant.

UNE RÉVÉLATION DE TRISTAN BERNARD

Tristan Bernard disait :

« Toute ma vie, j'ai donné le plus bel exemple de probité sportive : j'ai toujours donné des départs; je n'en ai jamais pris. »

Cette boutade n'est que l'expression de la vérité, car, directeur de vélodrome de la Toulouse-Lautrec (vers 1890 environ, où Toulouse-Lautrec le peignit sur le théâtre de ses exploits), le futur Tristan, alors Paul, fit un ou deux ou course à pied, en bicyclette ou en skis. Sous ce rapport, le Juif Errant semble avoir, à lui seul, épuisé tout le potentiel de la race.

Il ne s'est, d'autre part, jamais occupé non plus de sports désintéressés. Il était assidu au cyclisme, puis il le fut à la boxe, mais je n'ai pas souvenir qu'il ait quelque fois donné, à l'athlétisme, à la natation et même aux Jeux Olympiques de Paris, en 1924, aux joueurs de tennis-barbe qui suivaient ces manifestations.

La passivité de Tristan était normale. Les Juifs ne font pas de sport, c'est la règle générale. Pas si bêtes aujourd'hui, on ne peut faire espoir d'une compensation ou chiquer sans les quelques agaçés qu'on notera comme exceptions ne se trouveront guère que dans les exercices les moins pénibles, ceux qui procurent un maximum d'amusement

en échange d'un minimum d'entraînement.

L'austérité, l'abstinence, les sévérités d'un régime ne sont pas le fait du sémite. Il n'a pas se se fourvoyer dans les épreuves qui demandent un travail rigoureux AVANT et une énergie constante PENDANT. Non, pas de Juifs dans les épreuves de fond, que ce soit en course à pied, à la nage, en bicyclette ou en skis. Sous ce rapport, le Juif Errant semble avoir, à lui seul, épuisé tout le potentiel de la race.

Mais, sans se limiter aux exploits d'endurance, on peut étendre cette remarque à l'ensemble des compétitions sportives de première zone, qui, toutes, réclament beaucoup de ténacité et d'abnégation. Si l'on en excepte la boxe — sur laquelle nous reviendrons, et qui est à part parce que l'importance des gains oblige à écarter l'idée d'abnégation — on ne trouvera guère de Juifs qui aient brillé dans les grandes manifestations. On peut chercher, fouiller; compulser les annuaires, on n'en ramènera qu'un maigre butin. Pour notre part, malgré tous nos efforts, nous n'avons retrouvé que trois Juifs dont on puisse dire qu'ils ont occupé une bonne place dans le sport international : Abrahams, Hélène Meyer et Artem Natsche.

3 PETITS NOMS EN 2 GRANDS TIERS DE SIÈCLE

Un coureur à pied, une escrimeuse, un nageur. Pour deux tiers de siècle, en pleine période de résurrection du sport, c'est

piètre. Encore s'agit-il de trois champions, certes, mais pas de trois super-champions. ABRAHAMS, qui gagna pour l'Angleterre

(192) Antisemitic French booklet *Pitres du Sport*
[Clowns of Sport].

VII. HAVING FUN

(193) Cover and illustration of "Jews present them-selves," published by the *Stürmer*, 1934 (the naked truth, the rabbi, the beggar).

Siehst du im Osten das Morgenrot —?.

Lied und Vertonung von Arno Pardun

¶ 1. Siehst du im Osten das Morgenrot? Ein Zeichen zur Freiheit, zur Sonne? Wir halten zusammen, ob lebend, ob tot, mag kommen, was immer da wolle! Warum jetzt noch zweifeln, hört auf mit dem Hadern, noch fließt uns deutsches Blut in den Adern. :,: Volk ans Gewehr! :,:

¶ 2. Viele Jahre zogen dahin. Geknechtet das Volk und betrogen; Verräter und Juden hatten Gewinn, sie fordern Opfer Legionen. Im Volke geboren erstand uns ein Führer, gab Glaube und Hoffnung an Deutschland uns wieder. :,: Volk ans Gewehr! :,:

¶ 3. Deutscher, wach auf nun und reih' dich ein, wir schreiten dem Siege entgegen! Frei soll die Arbeit, und frei wollen wir sein und mutig und trotzig verwegen. Wir ballen die Fäuste und werden es wagen; es gibt kein Zurück mehr, und keiner darf zagen. :,: Volk ans Gewehr! :,:

¶ 4. Wir Jungen und Alten, Mann für Mann, umklammern das Hakenkreuzbanner, ob Bauer, ob Bürger, ob Arbeitsmann, sie schwingen das Schwert und den Hammer; sie kämpfen für Hitler, für Arbeit und Brot: Deutschland erwache und Juda — den Tod! :,: Volk ans Gewehr! :,:

Nachdruck mit ausdrücklicher Genehmigung des Verlages für Deutsche Musik, Berlin S 42

195

196

Worte und Musik: Herms Niel.

Als Soldaten Adolf Hitlers
Ziehen wir zum Kampfe aus,
Gegen Osten laßt uns fahren,
Niemand bleibt zu Haus, zu Haus,
Gegen Osten laßt uns fahren,
Niemand bleibt zu Haus.

Refrain: Lebe wohl — mein Kind,
    Denn im Osten pfeift der Wind, der Wind.
    Leb' wohl, Mütterlein,
    Heute muß geschieden sein.

Deutsche Frau'n und Kameraden,
Streitet alle tapfer mit,
Nieder mit den Bolschewisten,
Mit den Juden und dem Britt'.
Nieder mit den Bolschewisten,
Juden und dem Britt'.
Refrain: Lebe wohl — mein Kind.

Ladet eure schärfsten Waffen,
Streitet alle tapfer mit,
Siegreich woll'n den Feind wir schlagen,
Und die Welt hat Ruh, hat Ruh.
Siegreich woll'n den Feind wir schlagen,
Und die Welt hat Ruh.
Refrain: Lebe wohl — mein Kind.

Haben wir den Feind vernichtet,
Pflanzt nach gutem deutschem Brauch
Auf das Grab der Kameraden
Einen grünen Lorbeerstrauch,
Auf das Grab der Kameraden
Einen Lorbeerstrauch.
Refrain: Lebe wohl — mein Kind.

WE ARE THE STORM BRIGADE.

We are the Storm Brigade!
And up and down we go,
Of nobody afraid;
The first to deal the blow.
Our faces sweat with toil,
Our bellies faint for food,
Hands gnarled with bench and soil,
Grasp weapons keen for blood.

We are the Storm Brigade!
The class-war fighters, we.
In Jewish blood we'll wade,
And then we shall be free.
Leave words, which are no use,
Let Adolf Hitler lead!
Come, let us smash the Jews!
And then we shall be freed!

Our Adolf Hitler leads.
Come march into the fray.
No words now - only deeds.
Revolution starts to-day!
On to the barricades!
Only death can conquer now.
We are the Storm Brigade!

We are the Storm Brigade!
Revolver in our hand,
At our side, a hand-grenade.
We march on German land.
The Jew is terrified.
He opens his money-bags wide,
But Adolf Hitler will
Square his account with a kill.

SHOOT THE JEW-DOGS!

Do you know the peasants,
Hitler's marching host?
Soon the night will vanish,
To freedom! is the toast.

Load your guns with powder;
Load them up with lead.
Down with the Jewish tyrants!
Shoot the Jew-dogs dead!

DRIPPING WITH JEWISH BLOOD.

Storm Brigaders, young and old,
Take your weapons in your hand,
For the Jews have settled terribly,
In our German Fatherland.

There was once a young storm soldier.
Fate had marked him out for this -
To leave his wife and children,
And march without a farewell kiss.

The old women set up a howling,
And the young girls shed bitter tears.
Farewell, my love, my precious,
Farewell, farewell, my dears.

But when the storm soldier goes into the fray,
He feels it is ever so good,
To see his sword thrust and slay,
And dripping with Jewish blood.

5.110 cartridges in the belt;
And the gun is loaded, too;
And the hand grenade is ready in the fist.
Come here, you Bolshevik Jew!

194

(194) English translation of three German battle songs of Hitlerite youth. The text was provided by the Central Union of German Citizens of Jewish Faith and published in the English edition of the *Jewish Telegraphic Agency Bulletin*, October 14, 1931. **(195)** A song by Arno Pardun: "Germany wake up and to the Jew—death!" **(196)** Postcard distributed on the Eastern front: "Down with Bolshevism, the Jews, and the British!"

Das kleine Nazi = Liederbuch

Deutſchland erwache!

(45. Auflage)

198

25. Hitler-Garde.

Weiſe: „Zu Mantua in Banden".

Das Vaterland braucht Männer, es liegt in argem Streit. Erſt wenn die Juden ſterben, hört auf das deutſche Leid. Das Hakenkreuz weht uns voran, wir ſind der Hitler-Garde Stamm! :,: Heil, deutſches Vaterland! :,:

Wir haben auch erfahren die goldne Republik in unſern Jugendjahren, wir danken für das Glück. Das Hakenkreuz weht uns voran, wir ſind der Hitler=Garde Stamm! Heil, Flagge Hitlerrot.

Bald wird der Kampf beginnen ums heil'ge Vaterland. Wir neiden unſern Brüdern das Schlachtſchwert in der Hand. Das Hakenkreuz weht uns voran, wir ſind der Hitler-Garde Stamm! Wir ſtehn für Hitlerrot getreu bis in den Tod!

Und ſollte nicht gelingen der Sieg in kühnem Streit, ſo werden's wir erzwingen, wenn kommt für uns die Zeit. Das Hakenkreuz weht uns voran, wir ſind der Hitler=Garde Stamm! Es führt uns Hakenkreuz zum Siege oder Tod!

Nun, Deutſchland, zage nimmer, du wirſt nicht untergehn. Stolz blühn aus deinen Trümmern die Hitlerkompagnien. Das Hakenkreuz weht uns voran, wir ſind der Hitler-Garde Stamm! Heil, deutſches Vaterland!

Von J. R.

26. Sturmkolonnen.

Weiſe: „Bin ein fahrender Geſell".

Heil, mein Lieb, der Morgen graut, Tambour ſchlägt mit Wonnen ſeine Trommel dröhnend laut für die Sturmkolonnen. Weckt die Schläfer weit und breit in den ſtillen Gaſſen, nun leb wohl, du ſchöne Maid, denn ich muß dich laſſen. :,: Wir tragen Hakenkreuz und ſchwarz-weiß-rot ſtets getreu bis in den

197

Wenn alle Menſchen Juden wären ...

Ein ſchlichtes Volkslied zum Nachdenken.

Wenn alle Menſchen Juden wären,
Was würde aus der Welt?
Kein Acker ſtänd' in Ähren,
Kein Pflug ſchnitt mehr durch's Feld.
Kein Förſter ſchritt im Walde,
Kein Bergmann mehr zur Schicht,
Auch auf dem Meer zu ſegeln,
Behagt den Juden nicht!

Kein Dampfſchiff wär' erfunden
Und keine Eiſenbahn,
Kein Luftſchiff ungebunden
ſtieg leuchtend bimmelan;
Wir hätten auch kein Pulver,
Auch kein elektriſch Licht,
Denn Handeln kann der Jude,
Erfinden kann er nicht!

Zu unſrer Kranken Pflege
Käm' keine „Schweſter" mehr,
Und brennt es im Gehege,
Auch keine Feuerwehr.
Kein Rettungsboot flög' brauſend,
Wenn Maſt und Anker bricht,
Stets braucht der Jude Hilfe,
Doch helfen will er nicht!

Was kann der Jude geben,
Dem ſelber alles fehlt?
Im frechen Überheben
Sich ſelbſt nennt „auserwählt"?
Der Teufel mag es wiſſen,
Der Stolz und Hochmut liebt,
Gottlob, daß es auf Erden
Noch andre Menſchen gibt!

(197) Booklet of Nazi songs: "Soldiers, comrades, hang the Jews." **(198)** *The Small Nazi Song Book:* "Only when the Jews die will German suffering end." **(199)** Postcard with a popular antisemitic song.

199

201

(200) Antisemitic postcard by N. M. of Felsberg, 1933. "Don't buy anymore from the Jew." (201) "Out with the Jew," rules for playing a game for grownups and children. (202) A goblet with an antisemitic inscription distributed by the *Stürmer*, Nuremberg.

204

Sonnen-Aufg. 7.18 Sonnen-Unterg. 17.12 Mond-Aufg. 9.52 ● Mond-Unterg. —

FEBRUAR ★ HORNUNG

1763 Friede von Hubertusburg.

Michael Prätorius † 1621

Wenn's im Hornung nicht recht wintert, eiszapfet es an Ostern.

DONNERSTAG

Im Kampf mit den Juden.

Viele Jahrhunderte lang sahen die Christen den Heiland nach seiner menschlichen Art nur als Sprößling des jüdischen Volkes. Erst das Aufkommen der Rassenfrage hat uns eine neue Schau vermittelt. Unser, auch der deutsche Heiland, nicht in Judäa groß geworden, sondern in Galiläa, dem Lande der Heiden, in dem auch griechischer Geist stark wirkte, wurzelte wohl religiös im Geiste der Propheten; aber er ist der schärfste Gegner des Judentums, wie er sich vor allem seit der babylonischen Gefangenschaft unter dem Einfluß unduldsamer, herrschsüchtiger, engstirniger Schriftgelehrter ausgebildet hat.

Der Geist dieses Judentums und der Geist Christi stehen sich wie Wasser und Feuer gegenüber. Nicht aus den Juden holte sich der Gottessohn seine Gefolgsleute, sondern aus den Galiläern. Von Anfang an ärgerten sich die Juden an Jesu Worten und Taten. Darum suchten Pharisäer und Schriftgelehrte ihn zu töten. Johannes schildert uns im Evangelium besonders den Kampf des Lichtes mit der jüdischen Finsternis in der Hauptstadt Jerusalem. Mit ihrer Verlogenheit und Mordgier sind die Juden nicht Gottes-, sondern Satanskinder. Merke das Jesuswort:

Ihr seid von dem Vater, dem Teufel, und nach eueres Vaters Lust wollt ihr tun.   Ev. Joh. 8, 44.

Mai 1933

	Freitag
1521 Luther in der Reichsacht. 1923 Der Nationalsozialist Schlageter wird von den Franzosen erschossen.	**26**
1920 Hochverräter Masaryk Präsident der Tschechoslowakei.	Samstag **27**
	Sonnabend Sonntag **28**

Sicher geht diese Welt einer großen Umwälzung entgegen. Und es kann nur die eine Frage sein, ob sie zum Heil der arischen Menschheit oder zum Nutzen des ewigen Juden ausschlägt.

Adolf Hitler.

49

203

94?

KALENDARZYK- NOTATNIK

WYDAWNICTWO POLSKIE Sp. z O. O.

WARSZAWA

W 1939 r. żydzi stanowili 13% ludności naszego kraju, licząc 4.000.000 głów, ale czy wiesz, że:

70% prywatnego majątku skupiali żydzi,
95% kredytu zależało od dyspozycji żydów,
84% nieruchomości w miastach mieli żydzi,
88% przemysłu prywatnego było w rękach żydów,
93% obrotów handlu szło do żydowskiej kieszeni,
65% rzemiosła wykonywali żydzi,
87% zysków chałupniczych grabili żydzi,
36% było inżynierów żydów,
65% było adwokatów żydów,
62% było lekarzy i dentystów żydów,
75% było wydawców żydów,
72% komunistów rekrutowało się z pośród żydów,
100% handlu kobietami i dziećmi uprawiali żydzi.

Żydzi przynoszą narodom nieszczęście i nędzę!

205

STYCZEŃ—I

Bolszewizm i plutokracja to narzędzia żydów dla opanowania świata.

			8 9 10 11 12 13 14 15 16 17 18 19
1	P	Nowy Rok, Miecz.	
2	S	Makarego	
3	N	Im. Jezus, Genow.	
4	P	Tytusa, Izab., Eug.	
5	W	Telesfora, Emil.	
6	Ś	Trzech Król	
7	C	Lucjana i Juliana	
8	P	Seweryna, Teof.	
9	S	Marcjanny, Julian.	
10	N	Św. Rodz., Agat.	
11	P	Honoraty	
12	W	Arkad., Ernesta	
13	Ś	Weroniki, Leonc.	
14	C	Hilarego, Feliksa	
15	P	Pawła pus., Maura	
16	S	Marcelego	
17	N	Anton., Mariana	
18	P	Kat.św.Piotra w R.	
19	W	Henryka, Ferdyn.	
20	S	Fabiana i Sebast.	
21	C	Agnieszki	
22	P	Wincen., Anastaz.	
23	S	Zaś. NMP., Rajm.	
24	N	Tymot., Felicjana	
25	P	Naw.św.Pawła ap.	
26	W	Polikarpa	
27	S	Jana Złot., Wital.	
28	C	Manfreda, Waler.	
29	P	Franciszka Salez.	
30	S	Martyny	
31	N	Jana Bosko, Piotra	

2

MARZEC—III

„Żydzi są naszego kraju letnią i zimową szarańczą"
Stanisław Staszic

			8 9 10 11 12 13 14 15 16 17 18 19
1	W	Albina, Antoniny	
2	W	Heleny, Pawła	
3	S	Kunegundy	
4	C	Kazimierza Król.	
5	P	Euzeb., Adriana	
6	S	Wiktora, Felicjana	
7	N	Tomasza z Akw.	
8	P	Jana B.,Winc.Kad.	
9	W	Franciszki Rz.	
10	S	Popielec, 40 Męcz.	
11	C	Konstantego W.	
12	P	Grzegorza W. Pap.	
13	S	Krystyny, Leand.	
14	N	Matyldy, Pauliny	
15	P	Klemensa, Long.	
16	W	Cyriaka, Tacjana	
17	S	Gertrudy, Patryc.	
18	C	Edwarda, Cyryka	
19	P	Józefa Obl. NMP.	
20	S	Eufemii, Teodozji	
21	N	Benedykta	
22	P	Katarzyny, Bazyl.	
23	W	Feliksa, Wiktor.	
24	S	Gabriela Arch.	
25	C	Zwiastow. NMP.	
26	P	Tekli,Eman.,Teod.	
27	S	Jana, Damazego	
28	N	Jana Kap., Sykst.	
29	P	Eustachego	
30	W	Anieli, Kwiryna	
31	S	Balbiny, Kornelii	

6

(203–204) Antisemitic propaganda in German calendars, and **(205)** in a Polish calendar, 1943.

(206) Antisemitic cartoon in a Latvian satirical publication, 1943.

"Ať žije volná láska!"
Zednářsko=vědecké prohlášení:
"Není rasových rozdílů!!"
(Když není — tak není. Poznámka sazeče.)

"Já jsem Žid a kdo je víc?
Hloupý gojim neví nic,
jak ho pěkně za nos vedem.
Kšefty, válka — toť náš Eden!
Křesťan krvácí,
nám pro legraci!"

— — —

"Dodám vám vši, šavle, děla,
perte se — ať už je mela!"

(207) Antisemitic postcards, Czechoslovakia.

209

(208–209) German and Austrian Jews being forced
to wash sidewalks and walls.

208

211

210

(210–211) German and Austrian Jews being forced
to wash sidewalks and walls.

212

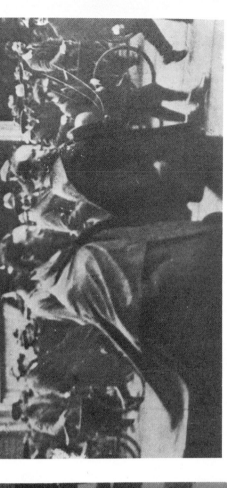

215

Humiliation of German Jews: **(212)** A Jew being paraded in an anti-Jewish demonstration. **(213)** A Jew being forced to trundle another Jew while the latter is seated on uncomfortable rungs of a ladder. **(214)** A Jew being paraded through the streets in a refuse cart. **(215)** Jews being forced to march dressed in the black-red flag of the German republic abolished by Hitler.

Immer vornehm! "Flottenmutter"
Berab. Kulant fährt an seiner neuen
Arbeitsstätte (Dreckwischen) vor.

214

213

217

216

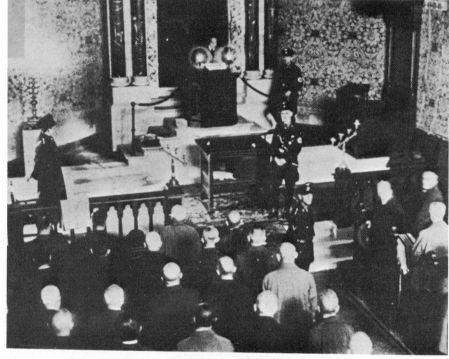

219

(216) A German Jew who dared to ask for police protection being paraded. (217) Parade of Jewish and non-Jewish internees in the camp at Sachsenhausen, near Berlin, in honor of Prof. Landra, chief of racial policies for the Italian Ministry of Culture. (218) Jews of Baden-Baden forced to march through the streets. The man in front carries a Star of David with the ironical inscription, "The Lord won't desert us!" (219) Members of the Baden-Baden community are forced to remove their hats in the synagogue and listen to one of them read the *Stürmer*.

218

222

223

221

In occupied Poland: **(220)** On the way to Poland to beat up the Jews; note the woman and child saying goodbye. **(221–222)** Polish Jews being paraded. **(223)** Jews are forced to run in front of fast-driving cars; note one Jew who collapsed and was shot dead.

220

225

226

227

(224–227) German soldiers in Poland are having fun by cutting the beards and side-curls traditionally worn by Orthodox Jews.

224

230

229

233

231

232

(228–229) German soldiers in Poland giving haircuts to Jews in the form of swastikas and Stars of David. **(230–233)** Humiliating Jews in Poland during the German occupation.

82

235

(234–236) Humiliating Jews in Poland during the German occupation.

234

236

239

238

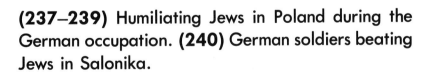

240

(237–239) Humiliating Jews in Poland during the German occupation. **(240)** German soldiers beating Jews in Salonika.

237

243

241

242

(241–243) Ukrainian antisemites humiliating and beating Jews during the first days of the German occupation of Lwow.

VIII. ANTISEMITISM THROUGH EXHIBITIONS

(244) Anti-Jewish panel at the exhibition "Das Wunder des Lebens" [Wonder of Life], Berlin 1935. **(245)** "The Führer's entry into Vienna started the exodus of all dark Jewish elements"; last panel at an exhibit in Vienna, 1938.

248

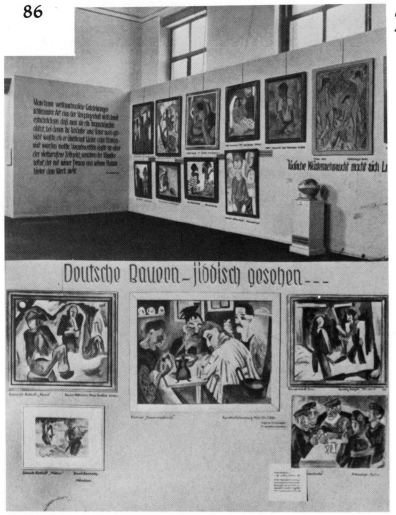

247

(246) The Berlin *Neue Illustrirte Zeitung* of December 1, 1938, published this picture of a woman looking at an exhibition on the expulsions of Jews from various places between 1276 and 1744. **(247)** An anti-Jewish exhibit in Munich claimed that rabbis drink the blood of babies, violate Christian women on synagogue altars, etc. **(248)** Anti-Jewish panels at the exhibition "Entartete Kunst" [Degenerated Art], Munich, 1937.

(249–252) Exhibition "The Eternal Jew," Munich, October 1937. Later it was shown as a traveling exhibit.

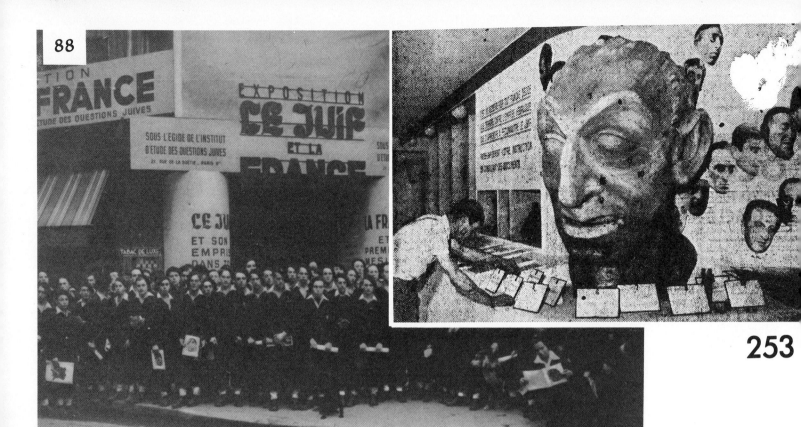

253

254

255

256

(253–256) The exhibition "The Jew and France" at the Berlitz Palace in Paris, 1942. (254) Members of the Kellerman Youth Center in front of the exhibition. (255) A Christmas party for children at the exhibition. (256) Posters announcing the exhibition in Bordeaux.

259

260

258

257

(257) The exhibition "Jews and Masons," organized by Francisme, the French pro-Nazi movement, 1942. (258) The front window of the recruiting office for volunteers against Russia; a sign warns Jews not to stop in front of the window. (259) Anti-Bolshevik and anti-Jewish exhibition, The Hague, 1942. (260) "Here are the Soviets." Poster for an anti-Jewish and anti-Soviet exhibition in Brussels, April 1943.

262

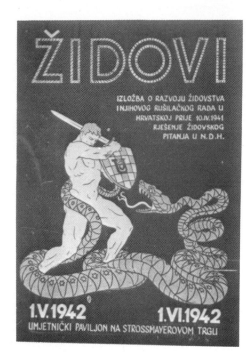

263

(261) Postage stamp commemorating the anti-Masonic and anti-Jewish exhibition in Zagreb, October 1941. **(262)** Poster for an anti-Jewish exhibition, Zagreb, 1942. **(263)** Poster for an anti-Jewish exhibition in the building of the YIVO Institute for Jewish Research in Vilna during the German occupation. **(264)** Poster for an anti-Jewish exhibition in Czestochowa (Poland), May 1944.

264

(265) Poster for the traveling exhibit "Jewish Infection" in Poland during the German occupation.

266

267

НІМЕЧЧИНА РОЗБИЛА ЖИДІВСЬКУ ВЛАДУ ПІД ЗНАКОМ
ПЕРЕМОЖНОЇ СВАСТИКИ ВИЗВОЛИТЬСЯ І ТВІЙ КРАЙ ВІД
ТИРАНІЇ САТАНИ.

268

(266) "Adolf Hitler, the Liberator of Europe."
Exhibition of ten photographs and one montage, with
texts available in Russian and Ukrainian. "He liberated us from the Jewish yoke"; made available by
the German occupation forces. (267) A section of the
traveling exhibition "The Jewish Plague," with texts
in Russian and White Russian. (268) "The Eternal
Jew." Traveling propaganda exhibition, texts in
Russian and other languages of the occupied
territories.

IX. "SCHOLARS" IN THE SERVICE OF ANTISEMITISM

(269) A few of the many "scholarly" Nazi publications against Jews. **(270)** The Mufti of Jerusalem, on a visit to the Institute for the Study of the Jewish Question at Frankfort, being greeted by Nazi officials. April 21, 1943.

LE CAHIER *JAUNE* 271

272

273

Attention ! ça brûle !

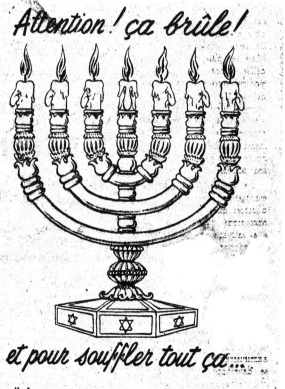

et pour souffler tout ça....

adhérez aux

« Amis de l'Institut d'Etude des questions juives »

21, rue La Boetie, Paris (VIII°)

274

(271–274) Publication, propaganda postcards, and a poster published by the French Institute for the Study of Jewish Questions.

(275) Satirical anti-Jewish publication of *Harc* [Combat], edited by Bosnyák Zoltán, director of the Hungarian Institute for Research into the Jewish Question.

STUDIEN-BURO STUDIJŲ BIURAS

Kauen, Laisvės Allee Nr. 41-b
Fernspr. 25428, 29668

Kaunas, Laisvės alėja Nr. 41-b
Telef. 25428, 29668

Als Manuskript gedruckt.

BULLETIN FÜR DIE ERFORSCHUNG DES BOLSCHEWISMUS UND JUDENTUMS.

Nr. 29

Kauen, den 25. August 1942

„Für das hungernde Litauen".

In Litauen wurde stets soviel Getreide erzeugt, dass es nicht nur für den eigenen Gebrauch genügte, sondern auch viel exportiert werden konnte. Das Getreide nahm im Export Litauens fest immer eine besondere Stelle ein, und wenn manchmal auch weniger exportiert wurde, so doch nur deswegen, weil der grösste Teil davon in der Viehwirtschaft verwendet wurde, welche sich wegen der Weltmarktkon-

schewisierte Presse. Die hiesigen bolschewistischen Zeitungen stimmten ganz unerwartet in den Ton der Sowjetpresse ein, und verbreiteten denselben Unsinn.

Nachdem die litauischen Zeitungen ebenfalls über den Mangel an Nahrungsmitteln in Litauen schrieben, wurde es den hiesigen Einwohnern klar, woher der Wind wehte, und dass alle diese Phantasien nur dazu dienten, um die brei-

276

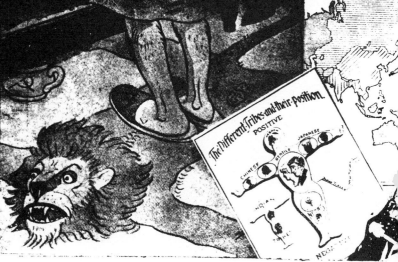

(276) *Bulletin for the Study of Bolshevism and Judaism,* published in Vilna and Kovno during the German occupation. **(277)** Title page and illustrations from *Yudaya Kenkyu* [Jewish Studies], an antisemitic Japanese publication, Tokyo, 1941–45.

277

278

280

279

(278) Berlin university students stand in front of the house of Dr. Magnus Hirschfeld as books of his library are carried out to be burned. (279) Transportation of Jewish books to be burned, May 1933. (280) Transportation of Jewish books to be burned, Hungary, 1944.

282

281

283

284

285

X. ANTI-JEWISH BOYCOTT
(281–285) Stickers calling for a boycott of Jewish enterprises.

GEGEN JUDA!

Nationale Volkszeitung Hof:

Nationalsozialisten!
Kauft nur in deutschen Geschäften!

Folgende in Hof sind jüdisch: . . . .

Sie schaden Ihrem guten Ruf
wenn Sie

in jüdischen Geschäften
kaufen!

Die Großeinkaufsgesellschaft xxxxxxxxx in Hannover beliefert, wie wir feststellen konnten, in unserem Gau folgende jüdische Firmen:

in Celle . . . .
in Harburg . . . .
in Bremervörde . . . . . .

aus Niedersachsen-Stürmer

Geht nicht zu jüdischen Ärzten und Rechtsanwälten!

Kauft nichts in jüdischen Geschäften!

Der Stadt-Wächter
Garantierte Auflage 17000
Unabhängiges Organ
nr. 20 · Preis 20 Pfg.
Mit der Meinung in Gott und Land
Sonntag, den 22. Juni 1930
Oberleitung

Unser Dienst am Volke!

Allen christlichen Käufern und Freunden des deutschen Mittelstandes empfehlen wir folgende

christliche, deutsche Geschäfte:

Fa.: B. . . . .
Fa.: C. . . . .

Folgende

jüdische Geschäfte

legen keinen Wert auf Empfehlung durch den „Stadt-Wächter"

Fa.: A. . . . .
Fa.: M. . . . .

(286) Anti-Jewish boycott. Montage in a pamphlet published by Central Verein deutscher Staatsburger Jüdischen Glaubens, 1930.

DER BOYKOTT

Meidet die jüdischen Warenhäuser!

Deutsche Frauen und Mädchen! Die Juden sind Euer Verderben!

Brief eines jüdischen Kaufmanns aus Schleswig-Holstein

Leider kann ich nur voll und ganz den Inhalt des Artikels bestätigen. Von hundert sind 70 Hakenkreuzler, 10 national. Geschäftlich leiden die Juden hier sehr. 2 täglich erscheinende Hakenkreuz-Zeitungen bringen täglich Inserate: „Kauft nicht bei Juden"! Es würde zu weit führen, wenn ich sämtliche Auslassungen spezifizieren würde! Bei jeder Versteigerung die Bemerkung: „Vom Juden von Haus und Hof getrieben!" Dabei hat weder Haus, Hof noch Bauer je einen Juden gesehen! Einzeln lassen sich die Hakenkreuzler nicht fassen. Gegen dieses Wühlen und Treiben ist man machtlos. Die Hakenkreuzler brauchen jedes Mittel, um die Existenz der Juden zu untergraben.

xxxxxxxxxxx

Kauf nicht bei Juden.

Kaufst Du beim Jud,
das ist nicht Recht,
dem Juden geht es
niemals schlecht.
Doch Deines Landes
Kaufmannsstand,
der wandelt an Verderbens
Rand.

Die Juden sind unser Unglück!

卐

Wir Nationalsozialisten
kaufen grundsätzlich nichts in Warenhäusern, Konsum-Vereinen, Kettenläden, Großfilialen und sonstigen jüdischen Geschäften.

Boykott-Handzettel

VÖLKISCHER BEOBACHTER

Herausgeber Adolf Hitler

Kampfblatt der national-sozialistischen Bewegung Großdeutschlands

Der Leiter der Greuel-Abwehr:

Schlagt den Weltfeind!

ner Ausgabe / Ausgabe A

Ausg. ★ 46. Jahrg. ★ Einzelpreis 15 Pf.

...mungen in der gesamten Presse

VÖLKISCHER BEOBACHTER

Herausgeber Adolf Hitler

Kampfblatt der national-sozialistischen Bewegung Großdeutschlands

Ausgabe A / Berliner Ausgabe

Berlin, Sonntag/Montag 2./3. April 1933

Ganz Deutschland
boykottiert die Juden

Planmäßige und wirkungsvolle Durchführung des Ab...
Ein S.S.-Man...

ganzen Reich

Der Fein...

Die Disziplin des erwa...

Nr. 77 ★ Freitag

Berliner illustrierte

Nachtausgabe

31. März 1933

...=Mann nieder

Volksmenge gerichtet

10 Pf.
auswärts 15 Pf.

Außerordentliche Maßnahmen
zum Beginn des Boykotts.

Termin bleibt: Ab Sonnabend, 1. April 1933, vormittags 10 Uhr

Der Aufruf der NSDAP.

---

(287) The press calls for an anti-Jewish boycott.

(288) Photographic report on the anti-Jewish boycott in Berlin, *Völkischer Beobachter*, April 2–3, 1933.

Zur Abwehr!

Am 30. Januar 1933 wurde Adolf Hitler, der Führer der deutschen Freiheitsbewegung, zum Kanzler des Deutschen Reiches ernannt. Am 5. März 1933 bekannte sich das deutsche Volk in einer wunderbaren Erhebung zu ihm und zu seinen Betrauungsport. Die

nationale Revolution

ward das alte System in Trümmer, und Adolf Hitler, der Marxismus liegt zerschmettert am Boden. Deutschland geht einem neuen schöpfen entgegen.

Dieser grandiose deutsche Freiheitskampf erfüllt den

Internationalen Weltjuden

auf! Daß sich an Grimm, daß er sich mit feiner Macht in Deutschland zu Ende geht. Er sieht, daß aus diesem Deutschland kann (und er keine sozialistische Betriebsführung mehr machen. Jetzt handelt er nach dem Programm, das der jüdische Abrüstungschef Theodor Herzl im Jahre 1897 in Basel bei einem großen Judenkongreß feierlich verkündete (Auszug aus der 7. Sitzung.)

„Sobald ein nichtjüdischer Staat es wagt, uns Juden Widerstand zu leisten, müssen wir ihn in der Lage sein, feine Nachbarn zum Kriege gegen ihn zu veranlassen... Als Mittel dazu werden wir die öffentliche Meinung vorschieben.“

Diese werden wir vorher durch die sogenannte „ädle Großmacht“, die Presse in unserem Sinne bearbeiten. Mit ganz wenig Ausnahmen, die überhaupt nicht in Frage kommen, liegt die ganze Presse der Welt in unseren Händen.“

Nach einem ausgearbeiteten Plan hat in diesen Tagen der Jude die öffentliche Weltmeinung gegen Deutschland aufgehetzt. Er bedient sich dazu der Presse, durch die er eine ungeheure Flugenlüge über die Welt erzielt. Kein Verbrechen, kein Schandtat ist ihm zu unbeträchtig, es bedingen sie die Deutschen damit.

Der Jude lügt, in Deutschland würden Angehörige des jüdischen Volkes erschlagen zu...

Der Jude lügt, es würden bösen Juden die Augen ausgestochen, die Hände abgehackt...

Der Jude lügt, Oberen und Bösen abgeschnitten, in Deutschland selbst jüdische Frauen vor den Augen ihrer Eltern vergewaltigt.

Der Jude verbreitet diese Lügen in derselben Weise wie er das auch während des früheres getan hatte. Er will das Zoeil gegen Deutschland aufhetzen.

Darüber hinaus fordert er zum

Boykott Deutscher Erzeugnisse

auf. Er will damit das Elend der deutschen Arbeiterschaft in Deutschland vergrößern, er will den deutschen Export ruinieren.

Deutsche Volksgenossen! Deutsche Volksgenossen!

Die Schuldigen an diesem wahnwitzigen Verbrechen, an dieser nieder-trächtigen Greuel- und Boykott-Hetze sind die

Juden in Deutschland

Sie haben ihre Volksgenossen im Auslande zum Kampfe gegen das deutsche Volk aufgerufen. Sie haben die Lügen und Verleumdungen hinausgemeldet. Darum hat die Reichsleitung der deutschen Freiheitsbewegung beschlossen, in Abwehr der verbrecherischen Hetze

über alle jüdischen Geschäfte, Warenhäuser, Kanzleien usw.

den Boykott zu verhängen.

ab Samstag, den 1. April 1933 vormittags 10 Uhr

Dieser Boykottierung Folge zu leisten, dazu rufen wir Euch, deutsche Frauen und Männer, auf!

Kauft nicht in jüdischen Geschäften und Warenhäusern! Geht nicht zu jüdischen Rechtsanwälten!

Meidet jüdische Ärzte!

Zeigt den Juden, daß sie nicht ungestraft Deutschland in seiner Ehre herabwürdigen und beschmutzen können.

Wer gegen diese Aufforderung handelt, beweist damit, daß er auf der Seite der Feinde Deutschlands steht.

Es lebe der ehrwürdige Generalfeldmarschall **Paul von Hindenburg!**

Es lebe der Führer und Reichskanzler **Adolf Hitler!**

Es lebe das deutsche Volk und das heilige **Deutsche Vaterland!**

Zentral-Komitee zur Abwehr der jüdischen Greuel und Boykott-Hetze.

gez.: **Streicher.**

Plakat Nr. 1

Druck Max Schmidt & Söhne – München

289

290

(289) Official poster of March 28, 1933, calling for the anti-Jewish boycott to start at 10 A.M., April 1, 1933, signed by Streicher for the central committee of the boycott movement. (290) People on a Berlin street reading a poster calling for the boycott.

Westdeutscher Beobachter

294

V
Amtliches Organ der NSDAP und
sämtlicher Behörden / Ausgabe Köln (Stadt)

Bekanntmachung!

Ich löse hiermit meine Verlobung
mit Fräulein Else Mallweg auf.

Denn obwohl Fräulein Mallweg meine Gesinnung kennt, kaufte sie ihre Aussteuer beim Juden. Doch nicht genug damit. Trotz meines Verbotes gab sie unsere Verlobungsanzeige auch noch zwischen Judenanzeigen auf und brachte hierdurch meinen guten Namen in Verruf.

Dieses alles zwingt mich, meine Verlobung aufzuheben; denn ich glaube nicht, dasz ich mit einer Frau, die bei Juden kauft und ihre Anzeige in jüdischer Gesellschaft erscheinen läszt, glücklich werden kann.

KÖLN, den 11. August 1935   Otto Füngler

Deutscher

kaufe nicht beim Juden!

Verzeichnis jüdischer Geschäfte
in
Württemberg und Hohenzollern

1. Auflage

Wolf, Isidor, Textilwaren, Friedrichstr. 17.
Wolf, Marga, Dr. med., Charlottenstr. 1.
Wolf & Sohn, Immobilien Hypotheken, Reinsburgstraße 33.
Wolf & Sohn, Lippmann, G.m.b.H., Kunstbaumwolle, Zuffenhausen.
Wolf & Söhne, Baum- und Putzwaren-Fabrik, Stuttgart-Untertürkheim.
Wolf, Th. & Co., Metalle usw., Unt. Birkenwaldstr. 31.
Wolf, W. & Söhne, Baumwoll- und Textilrohstoffe, Stuttgart-Untertürkheim.
Wolloch, Abraham, Salatöl u. Bodenwichsgroßhandel, Böheimstr. 101.

Wolsdorff, Zigarrenfabrik, Königstr. 12.
Wortsmann, Max, Baumwollabfälle, Charlottenstr. 27.
Würzburger, Jul., Metalle Maschinen, Cannstatt, Kanalstr. 32.
Zanger, Alt-Gummi, Blumenstraße 27.
Ziegler, Ignaz, Inh. d. Fa. Samson, Photographenartikel, Königstr. 68.
Zimmermann, jun., Weberei Königstr. 31 B.
Zippert, Max, Vertretungen, Johannesstr. 98.
Zloczower, Lothar, Dr. med. Stockachstr. 1.
Zündorfer, A., Weingroßhandlung, Rosenstr. 43.
Zündorfer, Ludwig, Dr. med. Filderstr. 45.

Sollten in dieser Auflage versehentlicherweise einige Namen von einwandfrei arischen Volksgenossen mitaufgeführt sein, so bitten wir um Benachrichtigung, damit wir denselben in der nachfolgenden Auflage Gerechtigkeit widerfahren lassen können. Des weiteren bitten wir um Ihre Mitarbeit und Bekanntgabe von weiteren jüdischen Firmen, die in Vorstehendem noch nicht erfaßt werden konnten.

Der Herausgeber.

291

Parteigenossen, Parteigenossinnen!

Die NS.-Hago hat die Geschäftswelt aufgefordert, Schilder anzubringen mit dem Inhalt: „Juden sind hier unerwünscht."

Ich fordere alle Parteigenossen auf, insbesondere befehle ich allen Parteidienststellen, nur dort zu kaufen, wo man Juden nicht wünscht. Diejenigen Geschäfte, welche diese Schilder nicht haben, und die also trotz aller Aufklärung weiterhin auf Geschäfte mit Juden Wert legen, können nicht erwarten, daß Nationalsozialisten in ihren Geschäften Gefahr laufen, mit Juden zusammenzutreffen. Wir überlassen gerne den Judengenossen die Juden.

Der Deutsche geht zum Deutschgesinnten.

Der Gauleiter: *Berger*

293

Wer bei Juden kauft, übt Verrat! 292

Die Erfahrungen der letzten Zeit haben auch hier in Prenzlau gezeigt, daß die beispiellose Großmut unseres Führers von den hier leider noch wohnenden Juden falsch ausgelegt worden ist. Die jüdischen Parasiten haben sich frecher denn je in Prenzlau aufgeführt. Ich habe aus diesem Grunde beschlossen:

1. Der auf dem Obermarkt zur Aufstellung kommende Stürmerkasten wird allen Volksgenossen zur Beachtung bringend empfohlen.
2. Wer bei Juden kauft, jüdische Ärzte und Rechtsanwälte konsultiert, übt Verrat am deutschen Volk.
3. Kaufleute und Handwerker, die selbst oder deren Angehörige bei Juden kaufen oder mit Juden verkehren, erhalten ab sofort keine städtischen Aufträge mehr.
4. Juden sind in Prenzlau absolut unerwünscht.
5. Die Rassenfrage ist unseres Volkes Schicksal und der Schlüssel zu unserer Freiheit. Darum sei jeder Volksgenosse, der Juden irgendwie unterstützt, als Judenknecht in unserer Mitte verachtet und geächtet.

Prenzlau, den 6. August 1935.

Der Bürgermeister.
Fahrenholz

---

(291) List of Jewish businesses to be boycotted in the Württemberg and Hohenzollern state. **(292)** Ordinance by the mayor of Prenzlau ordering an anti-Jewish boycott, August 6, 1935. **(293)** Order to put up signs on non-Jewish stores in Dessau that Jews are not welcome there, 1935. **(294)** Advertisement by Otto Füngler of Cologne that he has broken off his engagement to Miss Mallweg because she bought her trousseau in a Jewish store, August 11, 1935, Westdeutscher Beobachter.

„Kenn Dich aus…"

beim Einkauf in der Mariahilferstraße

Teil II.

Mariahilferstraße von Kreuzung
// Neubaugasse bis Gürtel. //

Dieser Plan verzeichnet sämtliche Geschäftsläden des angegebenen Straßenzuges und die Namen ihrer Inhaber. Die s c h w a r z gedruckten Geschäfte sind in christlichem (arischem) Besitz, die r o t gedruckten in jüdischem. Bei gemischtem Besitz ist ein roter Punkt vorgesetzt.
Gleichartige Pläne für alle Wiener Geschäftsstraßen sind in Arbeit. Die Erhebungen erfolgen mit allergrößter Gewissenhaftigkeit und Sorgfalt. Wer dennoch eine einzelne Unrichtigkeit festzustellen vermag, ist höflichst gebeten, diese dem Herausgeber Ludwig Haberman, Wien, 10. Bez., Riepelstraße 2 bekanntzugeben.
Mitteilungen ohne Absenderanschrift bleiben grundsätzlich unbeachtet.

Schottenfeldgasse
1

104	Blum & Haas A. G.	Linoleum
106	J. Ungar	Automatenbuffet
	Singer A. G.	Nähmaschinen
108	J. Spitz	Modewäsche
	F. Röthel	Kerzen, Seifen, Parf.
	L. Handl	Herren- u. Damenfris.
110	Mag. A. Seewald	Apotheke „Zur kaiserl. Krone"
	Bally	Schuhhaus „Corso"
112	M. Henenfeld	Strumpf- u. Wirkwar.
	Jul. Meinl Filiale	Kaffee, Tee
114	Löbl & Co.	„Lady" Strickwaren
116	C. Alexander	Stickereien u. Handarb.
	M. Riesch's Nachf.	Spielwaren
	J. Bien	Kürschner
118	A. Anderle	Handschuhe
	M. Baumann	Schokoladen
	J. Schwärzl	Rauchrequisiten
	J. Grohmann's Wwe.	Lack- u. Farbenhandl.
120	Stafa	Warenhaus
	Stafa	Kino [T]

2 +→

Kaiserstraße
1

122	„Hermes" A. G.	Schuhe
124	H. Brody	Automatenbuffet
	D. Melnik	Glaswaren
	J. Lang	Alles für den Schuh
	K. Löwit, C. Kollisch	Krawatten „Louvre"
126	P. A. Meusburger	Delikatessen
	Fr. Bernhardt'sSöhne	Uhren, Goldwaren
	Luttarotti	Tabak-Trafik
	Kollarz & Puhr	Herrenwäsche
	W. Baltaze & Sohn	Wirkwaren
128	Fr. Spevak	Herrenmode
	Postl & Steigberger	Café „Westend"

2

Neubaugürtel

Webgasse
45

Warenhaus Damenmoden	M. Stappler	111
	W. Schmetterling	
Handschuhe Damenmode Moden Kaffeeniederlage Bonbons	M. Gibian	113
	A. Ripka	
	Krupnik	
	Gebr. Kunz	
	J. Landau	
Ver. Gummiwaren Papier Drogerie „Westend"	Wimpassing	115
	F. Baumschabel	
	A. Mladenov	
Damenmode Damenhüte Wäsche-Erzeugung Damenhüte Photoartikel Tabak-Trafik Schokoladen, Bonbons Taschner	H. Schönfellinger	117
	E. Kunert	
	D. Coundé	
	J. Blaschek	
	L. Maurer	
	M. Leicht	
	A. Rybiczka	
	L. Haist	
	L. Hörhager	
Landes-Hypotheken-Friseur	Anstalt f. N. Ö.	119
	J. Ludwig	
Mod. Perlenschmuck Modehaus	Th. Hachlbauer	
	Schwarz & Fischl	
	[T] 64	

Stumpergasse
65

Warenhaus Hüte Café Kittner	B. Leitner	121
	S. Sucharipa	
Konditorei Fleischhauerei Viktualien Filiale Hotel Mariahilf	C. Schneider	121a
	A. H. Gabler	
	J. Rehak	
	Wr. Molkerei	
	F. Hahn	121b
	52	

Millergasse
45

Buchdr. u. Pap. Kurzwaren Likörstube	Hartenstein	123
	Hellinger	
	C. Schorn	
Konditorei Fleischhauer	A. Kuchler	125
	J. Tauber	
	L. Sauer	
Klaviere	A. Stelz	
	hammers' Söhne	
Tabak-Trafik Schuhmacher	H. Gomolka	127
	Fr. Chlumsky	
Café	„Patria"	
	J. Kinnsbrunner	
	29	

Wallgasse

Auf Anordnung der Kreisleitung der N.S.D.A.P. Gelsenkirchen in allen christlichen Geschäften zum Aushang gebracht:

Wir weisen erneut darauf hin, dass der Besuch von jüdischen Geschäften, Einheitspreis-Geschäften und Warenhäuser für alle Mitglieder der N.S.D.A.P. und deren Untergliederungen (S A. und S S, Anwärter, Angehörige der N. S. B. O., der H. J., des B. D. M., der N. S. Frauenschaft, N S K O V, N S B A G und N. S. Kampfbundes) strengstens verboten ist.

Es ist Ehrensache eines jeden Deutschen, seinen Einkauf ausschließlich in deutschen Geschäften zu tätigen.

Zuwiderhandlungen werden ohne Ansehen der Person mit Ausschluß aus der Partei oder der betr. Unterorganisation geahndet.

Dieses Geschäft ist rein deutsch!

Kreisleitung
Bunse, K. P. Leiter

295

296

(295) A guide of Vienna, with non-Jewish stores indicated in black and Jewish stores in red, December 1934. (296) Poster warning members of the Nazi Party against visiting Jewish stores, Gelsenkirchen, March 1934.

Wirf diese Zeilen nicht beiseite, wie Du das mit anderen Werbe-
sachen und Schriftstücken machst ! Ich werbe nicht zu meinem
persönlichen Vorteile, nein, ich will in dieser Gestalt für das
Bestehen Deines Volkes werben und kämpfen! Für das Volk, zu dem
wir uns in ganz grandioser, weltumwälzender Weise bekannt haben
Am 13.Januar! Gewiss, unsere Siegesfreude und Feiern haben voll
Berechtigung !
Aber Du vergisst in Deiner Freude E i n e n , der sich nun
hinter schwarz-weiss-roten Fahnen verdeckt und der weit schlim-
mer ist als französische Bajonette und englische Tanks, der den
Augenblick abwartet, da wir nochmals schwach werden, um uns zu
vernichten; der JUDE ! Das Gross dieser Gesellschaft hat uns ja
bereits verlassen und kämpft unerbittlich in verschiedener Gestalt im Auslande gegen uns.
    Du Christ, Du Deutscher der Saar; reiss Deine Augen auf,
    sieh' klar und nüchtern und erkenne die Gefahr !
Jüdische Aerzte, Rechtsanwälte und Kaufleute (Hütten- und
Grubenarbeiter findet man bei dieser Sorte Leute nicht, da
ihnen die Arbeit zu schwer und wenig lohnend ist) entfalten
noch voll ihre Tätigkeit, und Du gibst ihnen noch Deine sauer
verdienten Groschen.
    Du füllst ihre Kaufhäuser nach wie vor !
Du duldest es, Deutscher Arb
Frau, Deiner Kinder Mutter
Und Du, der Du glaubst, bei
zu finden, Du findest nur de
Rassenverderber, den Du füll
Vergiss nie ! dass die Juden
finanziert und die deutsche
dass Juden die Freunde von
auch noch sind. Dass die Jud
ster Grundsatz die restlose
Kirche bedeutet.
Vergiss nie ! deine 20000
die vor Deinen Grenzen blute
Gewissen, und an ihrer Spitz
der Jude !
        Vergiss nie !
Nicht einen Pfennig dem jüdi
so die Fahnen des Reiches i
schäftshaus-Fassade aufhäng
der Volksverderber und Zers
Meide den jüdischen Arzt, d
allen Angelegenheiten deu t
Anwälten deutschen Blutes u
blind im Siegestaumel des 1
        Du musst Dich e
nes Volkes, Deiner Rasse! Z
des Beispiel für das ganze
Dein Geld zu entziehen, und
Denke an den Grundsatz des

    " Ohne Lösung der Juden

Denke daran, dass der Jude mit der Lüge siegt und mit der
Wahrheit stirbt !

Heil unserem Führer ! Heil unserer lieben Saarheimat !

Bitte weitergeben !

298

1937

... wer vom Juden kauft
ist ein Volksverräter.

Wir warnen Euch noch mal im Guten,
lasst ab von den verfluchten Juden.
Es wär schon allerhöchste Zeit,
dass Ihr Euch mal die Augen reibt,
sonst könnt's geschehen,
man kann's nicht wissen,
Ihr samt den Juden werd' rausgeschmissen

297

(297) Flier calling for an anti-Jewish boycott in the
Saar. (298) Boycott flier in Upper Silesia, 1937.

299

300

301

302

(299–302) Anti-Jewish boycott in Germany.

304

(303–306) Anti-Jewish boycott in Germany. A night parade with torches at the Wittenberg Place in Berlin. An inscription on the window of a Jewish store reads, "Jewish pigs, down the paws."

303

305

306

309

310

308

307

(307–310) Anti-Jewish boycott in Germany.

(311) A sign reading "Jews Are Not Wanted Here" opposite a shrine in Oberstdorf, Bavaria. (312) Sign at Bad Tölz.

312

110

313

316

314

Wie das Mannheimer Rheinbad gesäubert wurde

Der Beginn des Auszuges der Juden aus dem Judenaquarium Bad Herweck, Mannheim

315

(313) "Jews Forbidden"; sign at the entrance of the imperial palace in Vienna. (314) Jews chased out of the public baths in Mannheim. (315) Sign, "The way to Palestine leads through the place." (316) Sign at an Aryan store decorated with Hitler's portrait.

317

Die Einwohnerschaft des Ortes wünscht keinen Umgang mit **Juden.**

320

Juden nicht erwünscht!

Das Kaufhaus hier gegenüber gehört dem Juden ← David Boas !

319

NORDSEEBAD NORDERNEY IST JUDENFREI!

318

Juden betreten diesen Ort auf eigene Gefahr

321

(**317**) "Only for Aryans"; inscription on a bench in a park. (**318**) A sticker with the inscription "The beach of Norterney is free of Jews." (**319–321**) Boycott signs.

325

323

328

327

326

322

(322–328) Boycott signs in Germany.

324

330

329

334

331

333

332

(329–335) Boycott signs in Germany.

337

341

340

338

336

339

(336–341) Boycott signs in Germany.

343

342

345

(342–344) Boycott signs on Jewish stores in Germany and Austria. **(345)** Sign on a Jewish bookstore in Vienna announcing that the owner is "in Dachau."

344

347

349

350

348

(346–350) Destruction of Jewish stores.

346

sind die badenden Juden in Breslau gegen jede
Belästigung geschützt

Der Eingang zur Juden-Badeanstalt

Sämtliche Bilder Stürmer-Arch.
Kennzeichnung einer jüdischen Gaststätte in Bresl

353

352

351

354

(351) "Only for Jews"; sign on a bench in a German park. (352) Signs "For Jews only" in Breslau. (353–354) Signs "For Jews only" on Jewish stores.

355

Zur ärztlichen Behandlung aus-
schließlich von Juden berechtigt
Dr. med. Max Bergmann
Sprechstunden:
Vormittags 9-10, nachmittags 4-5 Uhr,
Sonnabends nur vormittags
Fernsprecher 62388

Hannover, den
Podbielskistraße 337 I.

Rp.

356

Krankenkasse

Ohne Kassenstempel ungültig!

Das Mitglied obiger Krankenkasse
Herr:

Mitgl. Nr. oder -Reichsbahndienststelle
Geburtsdatum 23. 3. 26.

bedarf wegen

Berlin, den 27. Juli 1942 194

Nummernstempel 0271

Dr. Israel Alfred Singer
Berlin SW68, Prinzenstr. 71

C

357

Krankenhaus
der
Deutsch-Israelitischen Gemeinde

Zur ärztlichen Behandlung
ausschließlich von Juden
berechtigt.

Hamburg, den 193

Rp.

Klosterstern Apotheke
Hamburg
21. FEB. 1939

Dr. E. Orth
Hamburg, Colonnaden 18

358

**In diesem Grundstück
wohnen Juden.**

(355-357) Prescriptions marked "For Jews only"
and with the Star of David, Berlin, Hamburg,
Hannover. (358) Sign at a place inhabited only by
Jews.

363

361

359

360

362

(359–361) Anti-Jewish boycott in Italy. Sign on non-Jewish stores. (362) Sign on Jewish stores in Italy. (363) "Entry forbidden for Jews"; sign in a cafe in Normandy.

364

366

367

Juden im Park der Rue Lafayette in Paris
Sie warfen unserem Berichterstatter böse Blicke zu

365

368

(364–366) Signs on a restaurant and other places in Paris where Jews were refused service. (367–368) Signs on a restaurant and store in Paris reserved for Jews only.

Voici la liste des ███████ ales Maisons Juives,

gérées directement ███████ personnes interposées

qui exploitent ███████ oulation de Vichy

AGENCE-PUBLICITE.

SOCIETE SATRALUX, 15, rue Ste Barbe (Sapio).

AMEUBLEMENT

DEMEYER, 8, rue du Casino.
ELSTEIN L., 13, Avenue A. Briand.
ELSTEIN M., 9, Passage Giboin.
FELSTEIN D., 11, rue du Maréchal Foch.
KRNISBERG M., 13, rue du Parc.
LIEVIN Th., 8, rue du Casino.

CINEMA ET PRESSE.

CINE-PRESSE (Ginzburger), rue G. Clémenceau.
LA TRIBUNE (Ginzburger).

BAZAR.

PRISUNIC, rue G. Clémenceau.

BONNETERIE - TISSUS.

AU BAS IMPERIAL (Salawski B.), 22, rue
CAMI, 8, rue G. Clémenceau.
ETAM, 7, rue G. Clémenceau.
SEYMOUR, rue du Parc.
MAURICE (Tchoukrul), 6, rue Montaret.
MAURICE (Tchoukrul), rue Lucas.
WORMSER, Square Source Hôpital.
YVES, 10, rue Fornin.
VOQUES (Cohen), 14, rue de l'Hôtel des l
SCHOUQUER, 28, rue Burnol.
MOUTAL (Kowa), 7, rue Fornin.

CHAPEAUX

CHEMISIERS.

BARCLAY, rue du Parc.
LEINEN-PEUCH, Galeries de l'Hôpital.
LE MUGUET DE PARIS (Yaïm et David), rue G. Clém████

CONFECTION.

IRNA, 17, rue Fornin.
TELLA (Ven█████)███████

DENTISTE.

RAMA Michel, 13, rue Lucas.

FOURRURES.

EORGES (Abromaurich), 4, rue Royale.
ENDETSOHA, 27, Passage de l'Amirauté.
OBERT (Bendethsohn), 15, rue Lucas.
LIASCHEF, Square de la Source de l'Hôpital.
LIASCHEF (Grossmann), 24, rue du Maréchal Foch.
OTLER, 8 — A████ — ████ Wil██

370

Établissement réservé aux juifs	Jüdisches Unternehmen
ENTRÉE INTERDITE AUX NON-JUIFS	NICHT JUDEN IST DER EINTRITT VERBOTEN

WY, Place de la Source de l'Hôpital.

Vive la Révoluti██ ████tionale !

Vive Pétain !
Vive Doriot !

369

(369) Anti-Jewish leaflet published by Jacques Doriot's movement and containing a list of Jewish stores, physicians, etc., in Vichy. (370) Sign on an enterprise reserved for Jews in France.

374

Jüdisches Unternehmen
Entreprise Juive
Joodsche onderneming

372

NIET VOOR AUTO'S
BELG.GRENS 0.6
GEEN DOUANE
TEUVEN 2.4

TOERISTENBOND

GEMEENTE SLENAKEN
BEPERKTE BEWEGING VRIJHEID
VOOR JODEN
VERORDENING N-135-1941

GULPEN 6.2
HOOGCRUTS 1.8
NOORBEEK 4.3
GRONSVELD 13.2
MAASTRICHT 18.4

373

371

371–372) Signs on Jewish stores in Belgium. **(373–374)** Signs at places forbidden to Jews, Holland.

375

376

(375–376) Signs at places in Holland forbidden to Jews.

377

60. BEKANNTMACHUNG
DES STADTHAUPTMANNS.

Betr.: Benützung der Anlagen und des Alten Marktes durch Juden.

Das Betreten der Wege und Plätze in den Anlagen des Inneren Rings (Planten) ist den Juden ab 1. Mai 1940 verboten. Ausgenommen hiervon ist der Abschnitt zwischen dem Hotel Royal und dem Hauptpostamt sowie das Überqueren der Anlagen im Zuge von Verkehrsstrassen durch die Stadt.

Weiter ist den Juden der Aufenthalt in den Tuchhallen und das Betreten des Alten Marktes (Głowny Rynek) verboten.

Übertretungen dieser Anordnung werden streng bestraft.

Krakau, den 29. April 1940.

Der Stadthauptmann

Schmid.

381

Der Zutritt für Juden Verboten
Žydams įeiti draudžiama

380

Bekanntmachung.

1.) Der Jüdischen Bevölkerung wird ab 1. November 19.. Betreten folgender Plätze und Strassen verboten:
a) Adolf Hitler - Platz
b) Rathausplatz auf der Seite des Rathauses
c) Reichsstrasse von der Walowa- bis zur 1. Mai

2.) Bei der Reichsstrasse gilt das Verbot wie folgt:
a) Montag bis Freitag
von 13 bis 15 Uhr und von 19 - 5 Uhr
b) Sonnabend von 13 Uhr bis Montag 5 Uhr.

3.) Mitgliedern des Ober- Ältestenrates und Anwohn.. gesperrten Plätze und Strassenteile wird auf Antr.. über den Ober- Ältestenrat bei mir einzu.. ist. Ausnahmegenehmigung erteilt.

4.) Zuwiderhandlungen werden mit Geldstrafe od.. bestraft.

Radom, den 29 Ok..

Der Beauftragte der
für die Stadt
(-) Kuja..

Obwieszczenie.

1. Z dniem 1 listopada 1940 zabrania się ludności wejścia na nast.. place i ulice:
a) Adolf Hitler - Platz
b) Rathausplatz po stronie ratusza
c) Reichsstrasse od ul. Walowej do ul. 1-go Maja

2. Zakaz w odniesieniu do Reichsstrasse obowiązu.. następuje:
a) od poniedziałku do piątku od godz. 13 do 15 i ..
b) w sobotę od godz. 13 do poniedziałku godz. 5

3. Członkom Naczelnej Rady Starszych i mieszka.. zamkniętych placów i części ulic mogą udzielić.. kowo zezwolenia na ich prosbę złożona za poś.. twem Nacz. Rady Starszych.

4. Wykroczenia będą karane grzywną lub areszem..

378

379

(**377**) German order forbidding Jews to enter certain parts of Cracow (occupied Poland), including the market, April 29, 1940. (**378**) Sign in a Polish town forbidding Jews to enter the park. (**379**) German ban of certain parts of Radom to Jews, October 28, 1940. (**380**) Sign on Jewish shops in Lublin. (**381**) "Access for Jews forbidden"; sign in occupied Vilna.

382

EZEN HELYISÉGET!
POLGÁRMESTERI RENDELET ÉRTELMÉBEN
ZSIDÓK
LÁTOGATHATJÁK.

385

ВХОДЪ за ЕВРЕИ
ЗАБРАНЕНЪ

384

383

☆ ŽID ☆
MUDr. M. ATLASZ
LEKAR
LEN PRE ŽIDOV

Hungary during World War II: **(382)** Sign displayed by a small inn which was open to Jews. **(383)** Sign at the office of a Jewish physician who was permitted to care for Jews only. **(384)** The Star of David on a Jewish home. **(385)** "No admittance for Jews"; sign on a Bulgarian store during the German occupation.

386

387

Juden
nicht zugänglich!
Židům
nepřístupno!

388

Einkaufszeit für Juden: von 15—17 Uhr

Ausser den festgesetzten Stunden ist Juden der Zutritt verboten

Nákupní doba pro Židy: od 15—17 hodin

Mimo stanovené hodiny přístup Židům zakázán

389

(386) A Jewish store in Eger, Czechslovakia, smashed by local Nazis before the partition of Czechoslovakia. (387) Sign on a non-Jewish shoe store in Bratislava. (388) Sign in German and Czech on a restricted place, "Jews do not approach." (389) Sign in a Czech town stating that Jews are permitted to shop from 15 to 17 o'clock only.

Trade Guide

[Wirtschaftsfuehrer]

DAWA

German American Protective Alliance

Deutsch Amerikanischer Wirtschafts Ausschuss

OF THE

UNITED GERMAN SOCIETIES

OF GREATER NEW YORK, INC.

347 MADISON AVENUE

NEW YORK, N. Y.

COPYRIGHT 1934

392

Es wurde festgestellt, daß manche Fernsprechteilnehmer ihre Fernsprechstellen auch jetzt noch durch Juden benutzen lassen.

Die Postverwaltung macht deshalb darauf aufmerksam, daß ein solches Verhalten unzulässig ist und zur Aufhebung des Fernsprechanschlusses führen wird.

Jeder nichtjüdische Fernsprechteilnehmer ist verpflichtet, ein Ersuchen von Juden um Benutzung seines Fernsprechanschlusses abzulehnen. Auch die Vermittlung irgendwelcher Nachrichten für Juden durch den Fernsprecher ist unstatthaft.

Verkehrsministerium (Postverwaltung).

P. T.

Bylo zjištěno, že mnozí telefonní účastníci ještě i nyní dávají své telefonní stanice k použití Židům.

Poštovní správa proto upozorňuje, že takové jednání je nepřípustné a že povede ke zrušení účastnických stanic.

Každý nežidovský telefonní účastník je povinnen žádosti Židů o povolení k použití telefonní stanice odmítnouti. Rovněž i telefonické zprostředkování jakýchkoliv zpráv pro Židy není dovoleno.

Ministerstvo dopravy (poštovní správa).

(390) Order forbidding the use of telephones by Czech Jews. **(391)** Anti-Jewish sticker on a Jewish store in Bern. **(392)** The cover of a trade guide published by DAVA, a Nazi front organization in the United States, 1934.

Die Schweiz

Juden hinaus!

den Schweizern

391

394

STELLENMARKT

(393) Some German-Jewish communities tried to react against the anti-Jewish boycott by advocating the patronage of Jewish artisans. *Jüdisches Organ "Die Laubhütte,"* Hamburg, August 6, 1937. (394) Employment advertisements, "Only for Jewish or descendants of Jews Employers and employees," *Jüdische Rundschau,* June 17, 1938.

Kurorte und Gasthäuser

deren Besuch unseren Freunden nicht anempfohlen werden kann

Ohne Gewähr ∴ Auch teilweiser Nachdruck nur mit Quellenangabe gestattet

Abgeschlossen am 1. Mai 1931

Die mit einem * versehenen Orte müssen ihrer Bevölkerung nach als überwiegend judenfeindlich bezeichnet werden. Die den Ortsnamen beigefügten römischen Ziffern geben an, in welchem Landesteil sich der Ort befindet, und zwar bedeuten:

Ostsee (I), Nordsee (II), Norddeutsche Ebene (III), Thüringen (IV), Schlesien (V), Harz (VI), Sachsen (VII), Baden und Württemberg (VIII), Wesergebirge (IX), Hessen (X), Rheinland (XI), Bayern (XII), Oesterreich (XIII), Tschechoslowakei (XIV), übriges Ausland (XV).

Das nebenstehende Zeichen wird an nationalsozialistische Gaststätten vertrieben und soll anzeigen, daß hier Nationalsozialisten vorzugsweise verkehren.

Ein (G) hinter der Angabe bedeutet, daß sie dem im Nationalsozialistischen Jahrbuch 1931, Verlag Franz Eher, G. m. b. H., München, enthaltenen „Gaststättenverzeichnis für Nationalsozialisten" entnommen ist.

Der Landesteil, in dem sich der Ort befindet, wird durch Buchstaben bezeichnet. Es bedeuten: A = Anhalt, B = Baden, Bn = Bayern, Bg = Braunschweig, H = Hessen, M = Mecklenburg, P = Preußen, S = Sachsen, T = Thüringen, W = Württemberg.

Aach bei Oberstaufen (Bn), an der österreichischen Grenze: Pension Café Senwald. (G)

Aalen (W): Gasthof und Metzgerei „Zum wilden Mann". (G)

Ahlbeck (P) Seebad: Pension Villa Anna. (G)

Altheide (V): Villa Hannes, Haus Zahn, Haus Leopoldshöh lehnen die Aufnahme von Juden ab. Haus Schütting, Haus Helene, christliches Heim. Die Inhaberin legt jedoch Wert darauf, nicht als judenfeindlich zu gelten. Ilse, christliches Haus.

Amberg (Opf.). Gasthof „An der Wart". (G)

Amorbach (XII): Deutscher Hof.

Amrum (II): Nordseesanatorium.

Andernach (XI): Hotel Schäfer „Am Schänzchen", Verkehrslokal der NSDAP.

***Anger** (XII)

Annaberg (Erzgebirge). Restaurant „St. Privat". (G)

Ansbach (Bn). Fränkische Bauernstube. (G)

Arenberg b. Koblenz (P). „Hotel zur schönen Aussicht", Gasthof „Zur Traube". (G)

Arendsee (I): „Rheinischer Hof". Hotel-Pension Waldperle. Dreimäderlhaus inseriert: „Christliches Haus". Haus Burmeister inseriert „Ruhiges christliches Haus". Haus Sonnenschein empfiehlt „Pension bei christlicher Familie".

Arnstadt (Thür.): „Güldener Greif". (G)

Auerbach (Vogtland): Gastwirtschaft „Auerbachs Keller". (G)

Augsburg (XII): Restaurant Bayerischer Hof (nicht zu verwechseln mit Hotel Bayerischer Hof) legt auf jüdische Gäste keinen Wert. Gaststätte Schachmayer.

Augustabad bei Neubrandenburg (III): Kurhaus Augustabad. Auf Wunsch des Deutschnat. Handlungsgehilfenverbandes aufgenommen.

Aumenau (P): Gasthof und Pension „Lahngold". (G)

Backnang (W): Gasthaus „Zur Linde". (G)

Baden-Baden (P): Haus Feyerabend. (G)

Ballenstedt (Harz) (P): Försterei und Gastwirtschaft „Sternhaus". (G)

Baltrum (II): Hotel Kyper.

Bamberg (Bn): Gasthof und Restaurant Weiersch. (G)

Bansin (I): Haus Aegir: „Christliches und vornehmes Haus." Pension Runge: „Christliches und vornehmes Haus." Pension Margarete: „Seit 1899 bestbekanntes christliches Haus." Pension Dünenschloß: Christliches Haus. Haus Imperator: Christliches Erholungsheim. Waldhaus Eben: Christliches Erholungsheim. Haus Harald: Christliches Hospiz. Haus Rosenthal: Christliches Haus. Christliches Haus Inselfrieden. Haus Buchenhof: Christliche Pension. Haus Kehrwieder.

Bauerhufen bei Köslin (I): Hotel Strandschloß „Rein christl. Haus".

Bayreuth (Bn): Restaurant „Prinz Leopold". Restaurant „Frische Quelle". Café Wien. (G)

Bayrischzell (Bn): Müller, „Deutsches Haus". (G).

Beerfelden im Odenwald (P). Gasthaus „Zum Schwanen". (G)

Behringersmühle (XII) (Oberfranken). Gasthof und Pension zur Behringersmühle. „Juden finden keine Aufnahme."

Belgard (Bez.). Hotel Pommerscher Hof.

Benediktbeuren (Bn). Gasthof „Zur Benediktenwand". (G)

Benneckenstein (Südhochharz) (VI): Kurhaus Tannenwald inseriert: „Vornehmes christliches Hospiz", nimmt aber jüdische Gäste auf.

Berchtesgaden (XII): Haus Schöneck auf Gut Fischmichelleben gewährt Fremden christlicher Stände angenehmen Sommeraufenthalt.

Bergen a. Rügen (P). Restaurant Otto Schubbe. (G)

Berleburg (P) (Westfalen, Rothaargebirge). Gasthof „Winter". (G)

Berlin. Hotel Rheingold, Mittelstraße 24, gibt Lesern des nationalsozialistischen „Schlesischen Beobachters" Rabatt.

Berneck im Fichtelgebirge (Bn) (Kneippkurort). Gaststätte Merkel. (G)

Bevensen (III), Krs. Uelzen. Hotel Stadt Hamburg hat sich Gästen gegenüber jüdische Besucher verbeten.

***Bibra** (IV): Der Magistrat schreibt, daß er keinen besonderen Wert auf Reklame in jüdischen Kreisen legt. Café Reichhardt. (G)

Bielstein (Rheinland) (P). Hotel „Kranenturm". (G)

Binz (I): Haus Gäbel. Haus Quisisana, christliches Haus.

Bad Blankenburg (T): Pension Schreiber. (G)

Blankenstein (T): Gasthaus „Zur Eintracht". (G)

Bochum (P): Hotelrestaurant „Zur Krone". (G)

Bodenfelde a. d. Oberweser. Jng. K. Weickelharbt. (G)

Bögendorf (V): Gasthaus zur Hoffnung.

Boltenhain (V): Drei Kronen.

Boltenhagen (I): Haus Südwest.

***Borkum** (II) ist als judenfeindlich anzusehen, wenn auch einige Besitzer von Fremdenhäusern und die Badeverwaltung selbst sich in den letzten Jahren bemühten, jüdische Kurgäste heranzuziehen: Haus Dr. Pannenborg. Inselhalle. Pension „Constanze".

Braunlage (VI): Haus Weidmannsheil. Pension Elisabeth-Ilse. Haus Simon.

Breslau (V): Hotel Stadt Trebnitz. Gaststätte Berger. Café Opitz. Universitätscafé. Kaisers Café. Konditorei Bruno Laubner. Bauernschänke zum fidelen Gottlieb. Kaffee Geier, Gartenstraße. Pflaumes Gaststätte. Radickes Gaststätte. Klostermühle, Klosterstraße. Bürgergarten, Taschenstraße. Weidners Hotel.

Brieg (V): Hotel Goldener Löwe.

Brünnighausen (am Nesselberg-Saupark (Kreis Hameln-Pyrmont). Gasthaus „Zur Krone". (G)

Brunshaupten (I): Villa Barbarossa. Haus Glückauf.

Brüssow (P), Kreis Prenzlau-Brandenburg. Gastwirtschaft „Deutscher Kaiser". (G)

Buckow (III): Hotel Wilhelmshöhe, christliches Erholungsheim.

Büsum, Nordseebad (P): Pensionat „Siegfried", Logierhaus „Siegfried". (G)

Buttelstedt (T): Gast- und Logierhaus „Zur Bahn". (G)

Carlshagen auf Usedom (P) Ostseebad: Pension „Waldesblick". (G)

Caub am Rhein (P): Gasth. „Krone". (G)

Celle (P): Rats-Café.

Clausthal (P): Haus Hoppe.

Colditz (S): Restaurant „Zur Post". (G)

Conradswalde (Sommerfrische bei Bad Landeck, Schlesien): Pension „Zum Kreuz". (G)

Cranz (I): Oberstlt. a. D. Görschen: „Nur gebildete, christliche Mieter."

Cuxhaven, Nordseebad (P): Restaurant Lütts Ecke.

Darmstadt (H): Restaurant „Martinsglöckchen".

Daxenberg-Unterwössen (Chiemgau) (XII): Gasthaus Pension Daxenberg.

Deeb, Ostseebad (P): Pension „Joachimsthal".

Deeg, Kreis Zerbst (A): Gasthof „Zu den 3. Linden". (G)

Delmenhorst (III): Buschmanns Hotel.

Dessau (A): Kulmbacher Bierstuben. „Zum alten Dessauer". (G)

Detmold (III): Gasth. „Zur Rose". Gaststätte Richter. (G)

Deutsch-Krone (III): Kaffee und Konditorei R. Schmidt.

Dinkelsbühl (Bn): Gasthaus „Roter Hahn". (G)

Dittersbach-Neuhaus (V): Schloßbrauerei Neuhaus. Verkehrslokal der NSDAP.

Dizenbach (VIII): Kurhaus und Sanatorium. Prospekt enthält Vermerk: „Das Haus trägt christlichen Charakter". Inhaber legt aber Wert darauf, nicht als judenfeindlich zu gelten.

Donaueschingen (B): Gasthaus „Zur Sonne". (G)

Dorf Kreuth b. Tegernsee (B): Hotel und Gasthof „Zur Post". (G)

Dresden-Ebenheit (VII): Gasthaus Ebenheit.

Duderstadt i. Harz (P): Gastwirtschaft „Zur Stadt Hannover". (G)

Durach b. Kempten im Allgäu (Bn): Gasthaus „Zum Hirsch". (G)

Dürrheim, Bad (XII): Forsthaus Weilach Jochun.

Dürrheim, Bad (VIII): Privatkinderheim Villa Hilda. In dem Werbeschreiben heißt es: „Aufnahme finden christliche Kinder beiderlei Geschlechts." Die Inhaberin legt jedoch Wert darauf, nicht als judenfeindlich zu gelten.

Eberstadt (X): Gastwirtschaft „Deutsches Haus", ist Versammlungslokal der Nationalsozialisten.

Ebstorf (P), Kreis Uelzen, Lüneburger Heide. Café u. Restaurant G. Laue.

Edesheim bei Landau (Pfalz) (XII): „Zu den vier Jahreszeiten."

Eilsen bei Bückeburg (IX): Villa Ingeborg, Villa Schlößchen, Kurpension Hofmeister, jetzt „das Haus für christliche Gäste".

Einbeck (VI): Hotel zur Traube.

Eisenstein (XII): Gasthof Neuwaldhaus.

Elisenhof, Bahnstation Maltsch a. O. Jugend- und Freizeitheim „der nationalen Jugend".

Bad Elster (S): Kurheim „Prinz von Preußen". (G)

„DIE ERFOLGE"

POLITISCHE ERFOLGE

POLITISCHE ERFOLGE

Frick regiert in Thüringen

Im Freistaat Sachsen ist die NSDAP stärkste Rechtspartei

Im Coburger Stadtparlament regiert die NSDAP mit **absoluter** Mehrheit

In Gotha ist die NSDAP stärkste Partei

Maßgebender Einfluß im Stadtparlament von
Pirmasens
Plauen
Bayreuth

Die Folgen der Haß=Propaganda: 83 jüdische Friedhöfe, zahlreiche Synagogen geschändet

Gewalttaten begleiten den **Agitationszug der Nationalsozialisten**

Am 30.12.1929 wurde der Kfm. Richard Cahn in Alzey von einem Nationalsozialisten **erschossen**

Vom 1.1. — 1.8.1930 wurden 8 Menschen in Berlin von Nationalsozialisten **getötet**

Vom 1.1.—2.8.1930 fanden in Groß-Berlin 78 blutige Zusammenstöße zwischen Nationalsozialisten und Andersgesinnten statt.

XI. PROFANATION AND DESTRUCTION OF SYNAGOGUES AND JEWISH CEMETERIES

(396) Profanation of Jewish synagogues and cemeteries in Germany. Montage in a pamphlet published by the Central Verein deuthscher Staatsburger Jüdischen Glaubens, 1930.

Ibbenbüren

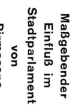
Jülich

Köln

Neviges

Essen

Ibbenbüren

Düsseldorf

Moers

Berlin

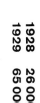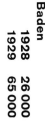
Düsseldorf

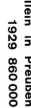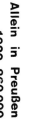
Essen

POLITISCHE ERFOLGE

Wahlergebnisse

Sachsen
1928 74 000
Juni 1929 376 000

Thüringen
1828 40 000
1929 90 000

Im ganzen Reich
1928 816 000

Allein in Preußen
1929 860 000

Baden
1928 26 000
1929 65 000

Mitglieder-bewegung
1920 64 Mitglieder
1928 **100000**
1930 Mai **250000** „

397

400

399

401

398

(397) Nazi slogans painted on the synagogue of Düsseldorf, 1933. (398) "This city is free of Jews"; Nazi slogan on the synagogue of Bromberg. (399) The synagogue of Magdeburg after it was dynamited in November 1933. (400–401) The synagogue of Baden-Baden burning (November 10, 1938) and the ruins of the synagogue.

405

404

406

402

403

407

Berlin synagogues destroyed in 1938: the synagogues of Augustrasse **(402)**; Prinz-Regenten Strasse **(403)**; Oranienburger Strasse **(404)**; Rosenstrasse **(405)**; Fasanenstrasse **(406)**; Levetzowstrasse **(407)**.

408

410

413

409

411

412

Berlin synagogues destroyed in 1938: München Strasse **(408)**; Markgraf-Albrecht Strasse **(409)**; Johanesstrasse **(410)**; Rykestrasse **(411)**; Lindenstrasse **(412)**; Lützowstrasse **(413)**.

über Stuttgart   Freitag, 11. November 1938 – Nr. 529 – Seite 3

Der gerechte Volkszorn übt Vergeltung

*In Stuttgart und im ganzen Gau Demonstrationen gegen die Juden / Die Synagogen wurden nieder-
gebrannt / Zertrümmerte Schaufenster bei den jüdischen Geschäften / Aktion in tadelloser Disziplin*

Als in Stuttgart und im Gau Württemberg die Kunde eintraf, daß der Gesandtschaftsrat vom Rath in Paris seit ... eine Sühne fand. Jedenfalls vollzog sich der Ablauf der Geschehnisse in einer eindrucksvollen Disziplin. Dies zu betonen wäre eigentlich für uns überflüssig. Wir weisen jedoch auf diese Tatsache hin, damit draußen, jenseits der Reichsgrenzen, nicht vielleicht jemand auf den absurden Gedanken kommen könnte, es habe sich hier um wilde Ausschreitungen gehandelt.

Jüdische Gemeindepflege durchsucht

Wie gesagt, die Synagoge in der Hospitalstraße brannte innen gänzlich aus. Bis in die Mittagsstunden hinein loderten die Flammen empor; die starken Umfassungsmauern des Gebäudes bleiben allerdings stehen. Nicht erfaßt von dem Feuer wurde das Gebäude der jüdischen Gemeindepflege und der Schule, das ja bekanntlich mit der Synagoge einen zusammenhängenden Komplex bildet. Die Feuerwehrmänner sorgten auch mit aller Kraft dafür, daß die Flammen von der brennenden Synagoge nicht auf diese Gebäude übergriffen. Daß man die Räume der jüdischen Gemeindepflege einer eingehenden Durchsuchung unterzog, ist wiederum selbstverständlich, denn wie wir ja von einer Razzia aus Berlin wissen, wurde dort eine erstaunlich große Zahl von Schußwaffen gefunden.

Brand auch in Cannstatt

Das Verhalten des jüdischen Schuldirektors war im übrigen auch so, als ob er ein schlechtes Gewissen

Juden haben unsere Langmut mißbraucht

416   **417**

415

414

German synagogues destroyed in 1938: the great synagogue of Frankfort **(414)**; Oppeln **(415)**; the Stuttgart synagogue burning, and a report in the *N.S. Kurier* of November 11, 1938 on the *Kristallnacht* at Stuttgart **(416–417)**; the Ohel Jacob synagogue of Munich on the morning after the destruction **(418)**.

418

(419) Inside the ruined Ohel Jacob synagogue of Munich.

423

421

422

German synagogues destroyed during the *Kristallnacht*: Oberfranken **(420)**; Essen **(421)**; Hildesheim **(422)**; Komotau, Sudetenland **(423)**.

420

Fränkische Tageszeitung

Nürnberg
Hauptgeschäftstelle und Ausgabeort Nürnberg
Zieglegasse 9 — Fernsprecher Nr. 43781/86
Postscheckonto Amt Nürnberg Nr. 5168

Nationalsozialistische Tageszeitung für den Gau Franken

Bezugspr. mtl. ℳ 2.– einschl. 25 ₰ Trägerl. Postbez. ℳ 2.36 einschl. 36 ₰ Zustellgebühr u. 46 ₰ Postzeitungsgebühr
Anzeigenpreis nach Preisl. Einzelpreis 10 ₰, ausw. 15 ₰

Nr. 185 Donnerstag, 11. Aug. 1938

Julius Streicher gab das Zeichen zum Beginn des Abbruchs der Nürnberger Hauptsynagoge

Eine geschichtliche Stunde!

Die Schande von Nürnberg wird für alle Zeiten aus dem mittelalterlichen Stadtbild getilgt

Nürnberg, 10. August.

In den gestrigen Vormittagsstunden wurde der Abbruch der Nürnberger Synagoge auf dem Hans-Sachs-Platz im Rahmen einer Kundgebung des nationalsozialistischen Nürnberg begonnen. Im Mittelpunkt der Veranstaltung stand eine grundlegende und richtungweisende Ansprache Julius Streichers. Die begonnenen Arbeiten werden bis zum Beginn des kommenden Reichsparteitages bereits vollendet sein. Das Recht zu dieser notwendigen Säuberung des ehrwürdigen Nürnberger Altstadtbildes gab das Gesetz, das Nürnberg in die Reihe der deutschen Städte einordnet, deren Ausbau und Wiederherstellung im Namen des Reiches geschieht.

Wer gestern in den Vormittagsstunden durch die Stadt ging, dem fiel auf, daß das Bild des einander entgegenkommenden Verkehrs verschwunden war. Menschen, Kraftfahrzeuge und Radfahrer bewegten sich alle in einer Richtung. Sie eilten aus allen Stadtteilen einem Ziel zu: dem Hans-Sachs-Platz. Und sie alle beschleunigten ihr Tempo, um ja noch einen besonders guten Platz zu erobern. Tausende und aber tausende waren gekommen. Wer irgendwie seine Arbeit auf einige Stunden unterbrechen konnte, der tat es. Denn diese Kundgebung, die Rede Julius Streichers und den Beginn des Abbruchs der Synagoge wollte jeder miterleben. So war der Platz und die anstoßenden Straßen von Menschen überfüllt, die zu den Zeugen eines geschichtlichen Augenblickes wurden.

500 Jahre zuvor, als in Nürnberg schon einmal eine Synagoge dem Erdboden gleichgemacht wurde, an deren Stelle dann die Liebfrauenkirche entstand, war es sicher nicht anders.

Erwartung lag über allen Gesichtern. Und als zur angesetzten Zeit Julius Streicher von der Insel Schütt her auf dem Kundgebungsplatz eintraf und die Musik zu einem Marsch ansetzte, da löste sich die Spannung in einem einzigen Aufbrausen der Heilrufe.

Julius Streicher dankte mit erhobener Hand für den Empfang und man sah ihm, der einst als ein Einsamer und Verlachter den Kampf gegen den allmächtigen Juden aufgenommen hatte, an, was ihm diese Stunde bedeutete.

Nun betrat er mit seinen Begleitern eine Empore, die vor der Synagoge errichtet worden war. Gleich darauf stand Oberbürgermeister Liebel vor dem Mikrophon und eröffnete die Kundgebung mit einer Ansprache, der wir das folgende entnehmen:

Oberbürgermeister Liebel spricht

Mein Gauleiter!

Volksgenossen und Volksgenossinnen!

„Als der Gauleiter von Franken, unser Frankenführer Julius Streicher, 1933 nach den Jahren des Kampfes im Nürnberger Rathaus mit der Führung dieser Stadt beauftragt hatte, da gab ich ihm und der

ganzen Nürnberger Einwohnerschaft das Versprechen, daß wir alles tun würden, aus dieser Stadt wieder eine wahrhaft deutsche

Fortsetzung Seite 2

Symbolische Tat

In Nürnberg wird die Synagoge abgebrochen! Julius Streicher leitet selbst durch eine mehr als einundeinhalbstündige Rede den Beginn der Arbeiten ein. Auf seinen Befehl löste sich dann, gewissermaßen als Auftakt des Abbruchs, der riesige Davidstern von der Kuppel.“ — Diese Nachrichten werden durch Draht und Funk über den Erdball jagen und mehr als einen mit innerer Anteilnahme geschriebenen Zeitungsartikel auslösen. Neben Stimmen des Jubels werden die ohnmächtigen Haßgesänge des Weltjudentums ertönen. Wieder einmal wird die ganze unflätige Gemeinheit jüdischer

Lüge und Demagogie auf Nürnberg und Julius Streicher konzentriert sein; zwei Namen, an denen heute in der Welt niemand mehr achtlos vorüberzugehen kann.

Ueber Mißbilligung und Zustimmung steht jedoch unverrückbar fest das Geschehen, jene symbolische Tat in den Vormittagsstunden des 10. August 1938 in Nürnberg. Was bedeutet uns der feierliche Beginn des Abbruchs der Hauptsynagoge durch Julius Streicher? Kurz gesagt: Eine historische Stunde im Kampf gegen die jüdische Weltpest! Wer glaubt, daß hier von Julius Streicher und seinen Kampfgefährten ein

Der Frankenführer spricht zur Nürnberger Bevölkerung vor der Synagoge, zu deren Abbruch er das Zeichen gab.   Aufn.: Hoffmann

(424) Destruction of the main Nuremberg synagogue. Report in the *Fränkische Tageszeitung*, August 11, 1938. The picture below shows Streicher speaking in front of the synagogue.

138

Viele Tausende Kopf an Kopf auf dem altehrwürdigem Nürnberger Hans-Sachs-Platz während der Rede des Frankenführers

Avh.

(425) The populace assembled at the Hans-Sachs-Platz during Streicher's speech.

428

427

426

(426–428) Three photographs of the destruction of the Star of David at the top of the cupola of the Nuremberg synagogue.

432

430

429

431

433

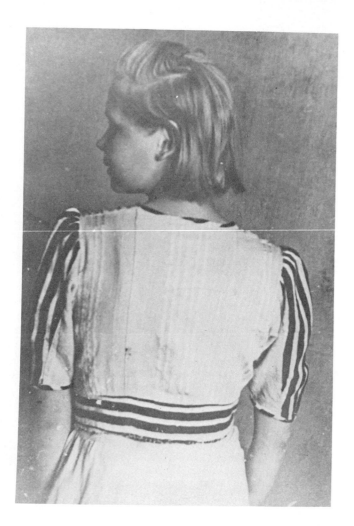

(**429**) The site of the former synagogue at Treuchtlingen. (**430**) After its destruction, the synagogue of Ellingen was transformed into a stable. (**431**) The synagogue of Gunzenhausen became a public market. (**432**) A cellar where goods confiscated from German Jews were stored; note scrolls of the Torah at right. (**433**) A German girl in a dress made from a *tallith*.

436

434

435

Profanation and destruction of the synagogues in Trieste **(434–435)** and Padua, Italy **(436)**.

438

441

440

439

(437) Profanation of the Paris synagogue at Rue de la Victoire during the German occupation. **(438)** "Doriot PPF" was painted on the Nice synagogue, August 1941. **(439)** "V = Vampire. Death to the Jews" and swastikas painted on the synagogue wall in The Hague during the German occupation. **(440)** Profanation of the synagogue in Apeldoorn, Holland. **(441)** American-Jewish chaplain at the ruins of the Luxemburg synagogue.

437

442

(442–447) The destruction of the synagogue in Antwerp (Belgium) on April 14, 1941: A group of Belgian antisemites taking souvenir photos (442). A Belgian with a pole on the way to break windows. (443).

443

446

445

447

The synagogue is burning **(444)**. The crowd is enjoying the spectacle **(445–446)**. The rabbi contemplates the furniture and prayer books thrown out on the street **(447)**.

444

Fuer Speisen welche man wegen Wuerner nachsehen muss, w. z. B. Salat, Spinat, Kraut, Blumenkohl u. dergleichen, uebernehmen wir keine VERANTWORTUNG

...TENBERG

448

449

(448—449) Two half-burned announcements of the Antwerp synagogue.

452

451

453

450

Ruins of the synagogues in Poland; the main synagogue of Warsaw **(450)**; the Gaon's synagogue in Vilna **(451)**; Kutno **(452)**; only stones remained of the synagogue in Wolbrom **(453)**.

454

456

455

The destroyed synagogues of Minsk, Russia **(454)**; Szekesfehervar, Hungary **(455)**; Cluj, Rumania **(456)**.

458

460

459

457

The destroyed synagogues of Bucharest, during the pogrom of January 1942 **(457)**; Sarajevo **(458)**; Nikopol, Bulgaria **(459)**; Nové Mesto nad Váhem, Slovakia **(460)**.

465

463

464

462

461

(461) On the night of July 27, 1927, seventy gravestones in the Jewish cemetery of Cologne were knocked down by Nazis. (462) Destruction of the Jewish cemetery in Rödingen, March 1930. (463–464) Swastikas and a hanging Jew painted on graves and the mortuary of the Jewish cemetery at Trebnitz, November 1930. (465) The slogan "Death of the Jews will solve the problems of the Saar" was painted in huge letters on the wall of a Jewish cemetery shortly before the Saar plebiscite.

467

466

(466–467) Destroyed Jewish cemetery of Diersburg and Schwerin during the *Kristallnacht*. (468) The tombstones of the destroyed cemetery at Coblenz were used for making steps. (469) Tombstones from the destroyed cemetery in Augustow, Poland, were used to pave streets and roads.

468

469

474

471

470

473

472

(470–473) Destroyed Jewish synagogues of Krasnik, Radymno, Siedlce, and Sarny, Poland. **(474)** The destroyed cemetery of Minsk, Russia.

475

478

476

477

(475) Tank-barrier made of Jewish tomb-stones at Miroslav, Czechoslovakia. (476) The destroyed Jewish cemetery of Saloni-ka. (477) A swimming pool made from Jewish tombstones in Greece. (478) A wall of the ruined cemetery in Riga served as a place for executing Jews.

INDEX

SOURCES

The American Hebrew: 181, 465
Der Angriff, Dec. 19, 1936: 33
Benjamin Arditi, *Yehudei Bulgaryah
. . . ,* Tel Aviv 1962: 137
Robert Aron, *Histoire de Vichy 1940-
1944,* Paris n.d.: 258
Elvira Bauer, *Ein Bilderbuch für
Gross und Klein,* Nuremberg 1936: 98
Dr. Ernest Bauer, *Die Entwichlung
der Publizistik in Kroatien,* Zagreb
1942: 41
Berliner Tageblatt, Aug. 24, 1938:
160
Bibliothèque Nationale (Paris): 271
British Museum: 4-5
Brussels Museum of World War II:
260
*Burgstaller, Erblehre, Rassenkunde,
Bewölkerung,* by Sepp, Vienna 1941: 84
B. Z. an Mittag: 89
Le Cahier Jaune: 255
Central Verein-Zeitung: 1, 396, 462-
64
Centre de Documentation Juive Con-
temporaire, Paris: 147, 437
*Le Combattant Voluntaire Juif 1939-
1945,* Paris 1971: 149-50
Corriere Adriatico, Dec. 17, 1938:
362
Current History (1938): 32, 38-39
Dr. Werner Dittrich, *Erziehung zum
Judengegner,* Munich n.d.: 86
Henri Faugas, *Les Juifs, people de
proie,* Paris 1943: 115
Fritz Fink, *Die Judenfrage um Unter-
richt,* Nuremberg 1937: 100-103
Le Francisme (Paris), Sept. 12, 1942:
257
Fränkische Tageszeitung (Nurem-
berg) June 25, 1938: 177; Aug. 11,
1938: 424-28;
Dr. E. Frenzl, *Der Jude im Theater,*
Munich 1943: 180
Front (Zurich), June 13, 1936: 24
Ab. Fuchs, *Tasnad,* Jerusalem 1973:
165
Grande-Bretagne—USA, No. 2,
Dec. 2, 1944: 442-47
Harvard College Library, Hebrew
Division (Cambridge, Mass.): 11, 16, 44-
45, 60, 169, 252, 283, 285
Hitler-Deutschland? Wahlen 1930,
Berlin 1930: 57, 286

Jewish Community of Bern Archives:
391
Jewish Historical Institute of Warsaw:
121-26, 130, 220, 222, 239, 264, 377-
80, 450
Jewish Telegraphic Agency Bulletin,
Oct. 14, 1931: 194
Judenkenner: 88
Juden Stellen Sich Wor, Nuremberg
1934: 193
Judentum unter der Lupe. Vöchent-
liche Beilage der Hessischen Volks-
wacht, Aug. 16, 1933: 200
Jüdische Rundschau: 117, 394
Khilat augustów, Tel Aviv 1966: 469
Kleines Juden-Brevier, Leipzig 1939:
113
Robert Korber, *Rassensl' in Wien,*
Vienna 1939: 80
Kranzler, Private Collection of Dr.
David: 188
Kublin, Private Collection of Prof.
Hyman: 277
*Lager-Verzechnis Ostpropaganda,
Lager der Abteilung Ost in Reichminis-
terium für Volksaufklarung und Propa-
ganda,* Berlin, 194-: 266-68
Leo Baeck Institute: 160-62, 355
The Library of Congress: 244, 248,
259
Matin, Le, June 15, 1942: 253
Munich, City Archives of: 418-19
Nachrichten-Dienst, Ortsgrupe Duis-
burg-Neudorf: 190
N. S. Kurier, Nov. 11, 1938 416-17
National Archives (Washington,
D.C.), T77 (1003-4647007):8, 54
*Nationalsozialistisches Jahrbuch
1933:* 203
Paris Soir, Oct. 19, 1940: 367
Le Pays Réel (Brussels), April 6,
1938: 21
Dr. Kurt Plishke, *Der Jude als
Rassenschänder,* Berlin n.d.: 81
Il Popolo d'Italia, Jan. 15, 1939: 361
L. Ran, *Jerusalem of Lithuania,* New
York 1974: 30-31, 128, 263, 451
Lucien Rebatet (François Vinneil), *Le
tribut du cinéma et du théatre,* Paris,
1941: 184
Rijkinstitut voor Oorlogsdocumen-
tatie (Amsterdam): 153-55, 172-73,
373-76, 439

Rostocker Anzeiger, Apr. 25, 1939: 49
Gerhard Schoenberner, *Der Gelbe
Stern . . .* Hamburg 1960: 153, 290
Morton Irving Seiden, *The Parade of
Hate,* New York-London 1967: 107
Savez Jevrejskih Opština Jugolslavije
(Belgrade): 134, 262
Statni Zidovske Museum (Prag):
386-90
Richard Wilhelm Stock, *Die Juden-
frage durch funf Jahrhunderte,* Nurem-
berg 1939: 3
Dr. W. Stuckart and Dr. Hans Globke,
*Kommentare zur deutschen Rassen-
gesetzgebung,* Munich 1936; 82
Der Sturmer: 22, 58-59, 61-73, 79,
97, 108-10, 112, 197, 352
Témoignage—Les Juifs . . ., Paris
1933: 186, 215
Ueckermundeschen Kurier, Aug. 7,
1935: 292
Völkischer Beobachter: 7, 250, 355,
370
Der Weltkampf, Jan. 1941: 178
*Weltentscheidung in der Judenfrage
. . .,* by Dr. Wille Fr. Könitzer and S.
Frunit, Dresden 1940: 40
Benjamin West, *Be-hevle kelayh,* Tel
Aviv 1963: 133
World Jewish Congress (London):
9-10
Josef Wulf, *Theater und Film in
Dritten Reich,* Gutersloh 1964: 169-70,
174
Würtemberg, City Archives of: 291
Yad Vashem (Jerusalem): 129, 131-
32, 208-12, 218-19, 310-11, 315, 317-
19, 321-25, 325-26, 328-34, 339, 345,
347-48, 358, 397-401, 406, 414-15,
423, 456, 458, 460
YIVO Institute for Jewish Research
(New York City): 12-14, 17-19, 25-29,
34-35, 91-93, 95, 148, 156, 159, 163-
64, 166-67, 182, 185, 191-92, 205,
214, 224-34, 237-38, 241-43, 265, 276,
280, 295, 356-57, 363, 365, 371-72,
402-05, 407-13, 420-22, 429-33, 438,
440-41, 448-49, 454, 461, 474
Maria Zelzer, *Weg un Schicksal der
Stuttgarter Juden,* Stuttgart n.d.: 415
12 Uhr Blatt, Jan. 2, 1939: 37
All other items are in the author's
possession.